HAIL MARY

HAIL MARY

BY DOM EUGÈNE VANDEUR

TRANSLATED BY JOHN H. COLLINS, S.J.

Imprimi potest: Gulielmus E. FitzGerald, S.J.
Praepositus Provincialis Novae Angliae
die 20 mensis Octobris, 1954

Nihil obstat: Eduardus A. Cerny, S.S.
Censor Librorum

Imprimatur: Franciscus P. Keough, D.D.
Archiepiscopus Baltimorensis
die 12 mensis Octobris, 1954

The *nihil obstat* and *imprimatur* are official declarations that a book or pamphlet is free of doctrinal and moral error. No implication is contained therein that those who have granted the *nihil obstat* and *imprimatur* agree with the opinions expressed.

New material and graphic design copyright © 2022 Silverstream Priory

All reservable rights reserved.

The Cenacle Press at Silverstream Priory
Silverstream Priory
Stamullen, County Meath, K32 T189, Ireland
www.cenaclepress.com

cloth ISBN 978-1-915544-13-1
ebook ISBN 978-1-915544-14-8

Interior layout by Kenneth Lieblich
Cover design by Silverstream Priory
Cover art: Mikhail Nesterov, Virgin Mary (1898), oil on panel

PEACE

In our *Abandon à Dieu* ("Abandonment to God"), a work which God's blessing has already circulated far and wide, we attempted a commentary on the Our Father. In that work we showed that, if we wish to taste the true peace which little children know, no prayer better manifests to God our complete abandonment into His hands than the Lord's Prayer.

The Hail Mary is the prayer of an archangel, of St. Gabriel, the Angel of Mary. It is in a sense a complement to the *Our Father,* if, indeed, we may say that there is anything at all lacking to that prayer which Tertullian has been pleased to call "the résumé of the Gospel." The Our Father contains everything that man's heart can desire or crave. And yet, even in the sacred liturgy of her canonical hours the Church scarcely ever separates the Hail Mary from the Our Father. The Office of the Blessed Virgin Mary offers many examples. Such action shows us in what extraordinary esteem the Church holds this prayer. From the beginning of the Christian era she has recognized in its makeup a kind of "synthesis of Marian theology," so beautiful, so profound, that she urges every one of the faithful who meditates on and says the Hail Mary to surrender himself in complete and genuine abandonment to her who, because she is the Mother of God, is of necessity the Mother of men. The Hail Mary, carefully studied and well understood, leads the Christian soul without fail along the "way of confidence" and reinforces still more the "way of peace."

This work is in no way a treatise on Marian theology, but it does find its inspiration in the facts of Holy Writ and the writings of the Fathers and Doctors of the Church, making use of all that they teach us about devotion to Mary.

To aid the reader and help him go to Mary, we shall retain the method followed in a similar work. We shall examine each word or phrase of the Hail Mary and extract from its meaning thoughts that nourish the mind and feelings that expand the heart. Let each one take what he wishes, each for his own need, each in his own measure. We shall proceed slowly, in order to digest that "Secret of Mary," wherein we contemplate the "Secret of Jesus."

Meditation on the Angelic Salutation helps singularly in the practice of praying the Holy Rosary, a practice becoming daily better understood. It should call forth in the heart that delights in it a more admirable, more confident love of Mary, an attachment more complete to her of whom was born Jesus, who is called Christ.[1]

These pages, we should say, pretend to nothing else. In the great concert of praise which ancient and modern writers (how many of them renowned!) dedicate to Mary, they would seem, perhaps, a puny offering. But, after all, she who directs that heavenly and virginal symphony has never refused the presence of any latecomer whatsoever, who makes his humble contribution. The little shepherd's pipe also has its charm, and the Spouse of the Holy Spirit is always sufficiently inspired to mingle and blend its rustic melody with the masterly and rich combinations of most solemn harmony. It happens, even, that the little pipe captivates your artists.

At the outset I ask of the Virgin, whom Gabriel saluted, pardon for the least unwitting false note that may escape my artless instrument.

THE AUTHOR

---

[1] St. Matt. 1:16.

PREFACE

ONE of the most illustrious servants of Mary, St. Grignon de Montfort, has written:

"O predestinate souls, slaves of Jesus in Mary, learn that the Hail Mary is the most beautiful of all prayers after the Our Father. It is the most perfect compliment which you can make to Mary, because it is the compliment which the Most High sent her by an archangel, in order to win her heart; and it was so powerful over her heart by the secret charms of which it is so full, that in spite of her profound humility she gave her consent to the Incarnation of the Word. It is by this compliment also that you will infallibly win her heart, if you say it as you ought.

"The Hail Mary well said—that is, with attention, devotion, and modesty—is, according to the saints, the enemy of the devil which puts him to flight, and the hammer which crushes him. It is the sanctification of the soul, the joy of the angels, the melody of the predestinate, the canticle of the New Testament, the pleasure of Mary, and the glory of the most Holy Trinity. The Hail Mary is a heavenly dew which fertilizes the soul. It is the chaste and loving kiss which we give to Mary. It is a vermilion rose which we present to her; a precious pearl we offer her; a chalice of divine ambrosial nectar which we proffer to her. All these are comparisons of the saints."[2]

---

[2] *True Devotion to the Blessed Virgin Mary*, translated from the French by Frederick William Faber, D.D. Revised Edition, 1950. The Montfort Fathers' Publications, pp. 185–186. Reprinted with permission.

We may add that to Mary the Angelic Salutation seemed so great, so extraordinary a thing that, as St. Luke tells us, the Virgin herself gave it serious consideration. She pondered it and weighed the cost. She "thought with herself what manner of salutation this should be."[3]

May that Blessed Mother of God, ever Virgin, help us to sound aright the mysteries of the Hail Mary! Then, and only then, enraptured by such beauty, shall we love to recite it properly. A single Hail Mary well said is worth a hundred or a thousand others said carelessly or with distraction.

Finally, do not forget, Christian soul, that you will never greet Mary thus properly, without receiving her admirable greeting in return. If you say the Hail Mary devoutly a thousand times, she will return your greeting a thousand times. And remember, from the greeting that Mary gives comes the flood of grace of which Gabriel declares her full. And so, before perusing these pages, say to her again:

Hail, Mary! full of grace, the Lord is with thee; blessed art thou among women, and blessed is the fruit of thy womb, Jesus.

Holy Mary, Mother of God, pray for us sinners, now and at the hour of our death. Amen.

---

3 St. Luke 1:29.

DEDICATION
TO THE
MOST BLESSED VIRGIN MARY,
MOTHER OF GOD

I COME to prostrate myself before thee, august Queen of heaven and earth, and to render thee the most respectful homage of my mind and heart. I come to lay at thy feet these few pages, before presenting them to the eyes of thy servants. Most humbly do I pray thee to accept them as thine own. Moreover, I charge all who may read them to consider them thine.

Thou hast a right, most Holy Virgin, to every word spoken or written by man in time, since thou hast given men the Father's eternal Word, and since through thee alone He has spoken by His Word in outward form.

Thou hast equally a right to all men's thoughts, since through thee all men have received the eternal Thought or Concept whom we call His only Son, in whom are hidden all the treasures of divine wisdom.

Not only hast thou a right to man's every word and thought, but thou hast a lawful and very special right to every book written or printed in any part of the Christian world. They are all thine. They should be dedicated to thee, who art thyself "the book of the generation of Jesus Christ,"[4] the Son of God.

If, then, every book is thine, hast thou not every right to this? One has but to glance at its title and title-page to admit

---

4 St. Matt. 1:1.

that it is thine and that in justice it belongs to thee.

Deign, then, to accept, most amiable Mother of my Saviour, this my tiny mark of homage, whose whole merit springs from its subject matter. Only my confidence, so often sustained by marks of thy protection, prompts me to undertake the task. What a happiness for me, if it succeeds in pleasing thee!

I know that it deserves only scorn and rebuff, when it has but corruption for the source from which it flows. When I recall that so many great saints trembled with fear at sight of thee and deemed themselves unworthy to write or speak of thine unutterable privileges, I am not afraid here sincerely to confess my rashness.

I am confounded in thy presence, august Mother of God, and I ask myself: who am I to dare undertake what so many illustrious writers and so many great saints confessed to be beyond their strength?

But, encouraged by St. Bernard's words and sentiments, in spite of my unworthiness and inability, I wish, most Blessed Virgin, to think of thee; I wish to speak of thee, to write of thee; I wish never to cease from honoring thee; I wish to bend my every effort towards winning all to dedicate their whole hearts to thee and to proclaim themselves openly thy servants and devotees.

Give to this little book the mission and commission to go and preach thee everywhere and win every heart to thee. To that end I leave it at thy feet and beg thy blessing with these final words:

> Let me praise thee, sainted Virgin,
> Grant me strength against thy foes![5]

---

5 We borrow this "Dedication," which so perfectly expresses our sentiments, from an author of the 17th century, Rev. Louis-François d'Argenton, Cap., in *Conférences théologiques et spirituelles sur les Grandeurs de la Sainte Vierge Marie, Mère de Dieu*, a work with many claims to greatness.

CONTENTS

Peace ~ v
Preface ~ vii
Dedication to the Most Blessed Virgin Mary,
    Mother of God ~ ix
The Hail Mary ~ 1

Introduction: Annunciation: Setting and Commentary ~ 3
    The Angel of the Ave
    Gabriel Appears
    The Virgin is Troubled
    The Blessed of the Holy Spirit

Part One: The Angelic Salutation ~ 19
    Ave ... Hail ~ 21
        Glory of the Ave

    Mary ~ 25
        The Name All Beautiful

    Full of Grace ~ 29
        Her Beauty
        Sanctifying Grace
        The Immaculate One
        Fulness of Grace
        Mediatrix

    The Lord Is With Thee ~ 43
        The Predestined One

    Magnificat
    The Fruitful Spring

Blessed Art Thou Among Women ~ 55

Blessed is the Fruit of Thy Womb, Jesus ~ 63
    The Visitation
    Elizabeth's Salutation

Jesus ~ 75
    The Name Above All Names
    The Power of That Name

Part Two: The Invocation ~ 85

Holy Mary ~ 87
    Her Holiness
    Her Virtues

Mother of God ~ 95
    Her Virginity
    The Great Mystery
    The Wonder of Men

Pray For Us ~ 111
    All-Powerful Suppliant

Sinners ~ 117
    Mother of Mercy

Now ~ 125
    Now and For Ever

And at the Hour of Our Death ~ 131

Amen ~ 139

HAIL MARY!
FULL OF GRACE,
THE LORD IS WITH THEE;
BLESSED ART THOU AMONG WOMEN
AND
BLESSED IS THE FRUIT OF THY WOMB,
JESUS.
HOLY MARY, MOTHER OF GOD,
PRAY FOR US SINNERS,
NOW AND AT THE
HOUR OF OUR DEATH.
AMEN.

1. THE ANGEL OF THE AVE

It will be your everlasting glory, holy archangel Gabriel, to have been the first to utter on earth the *Ave Maria,* the *Salutation* to Mary, Mother of God, Virgin of virgins.

You seem to be the Angel of the Incarnation, the Angel of that mystery so sublime that God will employ all the might of His arm to accomplish it.

Your name, in fact, signifies the might of God. Is it not yours to announce God's noble handiwork? It signifies, also, God-Man. Is it not the epitome of that tremendous mystery?

The Salutation was delivered in eternity, at the council of the adorable Trinity, which hailed Mary before the beginning of time. You were delegated to bear it down to earth.

As you deliver the Salutation to that Virgin, the Immaculate One, the whole universe from highest heaven to the depths of hell will be shaken. It is the superabundant outpouring of God's Heart.

In it heaven will witness the prelude of the incomprehensible mystery of a God who clothes Himself in flesh, a mystery in which the majesty of God empties itself, in which God becomes mortal in order to render man immortal.

Earth will leap with the joy of it, anticipating the dawn of the incomparable mystery of its redemption, the mystery in which God gives His life to save men and to restore them to the freedom of the elect.

In it hell and its demons will feel the dread presence of the

Almighty One, who comes to destroy their empire. The demons quake with terror. Nothing can affright them like the sound of that Salutation.

What a momentous errand, that on which you are dispatched, Gabriel! The more momentous, since it deals with "the event of the ages," with God's interests, with the concerns of heaven and earth.

It is the concern of men, of all who have dwelt or will dwell on earth from the creation of the world to the end of time.

That concern is not for temporal goods, for fleeting honor or even for life that passes away; it is a matter of infinite good or evil, of unending glory or shame, of life-or-death everlasting.

The angels themselves have an interest in that Salutation about to be uttered. So many of them, in Lucifer's train, have beheld their nature ruined, their place in heaven lost, and themselves cast headlong into endless damnation.

The vacant places must be filled. Now, only men can occupy them. The angels know well that to mere man that is impossible, but not impossible to God.

The Salutation is about to announce that God is descending to earth to effect man's ascent to heaven. The damage will be repaired. Only God, become man in wondrous wise, can make angels of men.

Chiefly concerned with that mystery is God Himself, who desires to make peace between heaven and earth, between Himself and mankind, at war with Him almost from the beginning.

Gabriel's Salutation is about to seal the marriage contract which will cause the two natures, the divine and the human, to enter into an alliance so close that they will belong to only one Person, the God-Man.

From the conclusion of that grand event will depend man's eternal happiness. In close relation to it stand the angels' perfection and beatitude, and the total glory which God receives from His creatures.

Go, then, holy archangel, go and bring to the Virgin Mary the Blessed Trinity's eternal and ineffable message! Make your way through the boundless space separating heaven from earth!

She lives at Nazareth, the "city of flowers." The circumference of its encircling walls is narrow; small the house in which she dwells; but around it lies the whole range of the Kingdom of Heaven.

Go in haste! Tell her that the hour of God's mercy has arrived. Go tell her that she is so pleasing to God that it has been decreed that she will be the Mother of His only Son.

Forsake for a moment your exalted station in heaven. Ambassador of the infinite God, take as your retinue legions of the nine hallowed hierarchies of angels. In such pomp and splendor advance, press on!

In guise of a man noble, masterful, majestic enter the secret chamber of the admirable Virgin, whom you will find alone.

God clothes you in such beauty, such splendor, that you outshine every visible earthly being; by that sign the Immaculate One will know that you are a prince from heaven.

The Virgin, lowly, rapt in Him whom she adores in you, will listen as to God Himself, especially since He alone has been able to compose and prepare your sublime address.

You must add nothing, change not a word of it. You are not about to reveal your own thought, but that of the Almighty Monarch who sends you and speaks through your lips.

The message which you are about to utter will enter into Mary. She will take it as coming from the lips of God who draws nigh.

Speak, then, holy angel! Heaven and earth are waiting and already tremble with emotion. That we may learn who she is, deliver to Mary the Salutation of time and eternity.

2. GABRIEL APPEARS

Holy archangel, you need not knock at Mary's door to have it open to you. Never a sound do you make to warn that you are entering with full right as ambassador of the world's Monarch.

Locks cannot stay you; by virtue of your nature you penetrate everywhere. To men, not to angels, does a virgin shut her door.[1]

Good angel, you enter the virginal room in borrowed human form, agile and airy, as spirits are. You present yourself in silence, in deep humility, not to receive, but to give.

In performing the office of ambassador of the Most High, you keep intact the authority and the majesty of the Lord whom you represent. With becoming dignity, standing up, you speak to the Virgin.

She, who never rises from the depths of her nothingness, who will one day sing of the lowliness of the Lord's handmaid, now rises out of respect for God's messenger.

And yet, who here excels in nobility, in eminence, you or she? Not an instant do you hesitate. The Salutation which you are about to deliver is an admission of your loving vassalage.

Behold! a thing never before seen. Until now human beings have deemed it a supreme honor to reverence angels; to that the Virgin's trembling openly bears witness.

An angel, in fact, does not show reverence to man, because he is nobler than man; in dignity he is man's superior. An angel is a spiritual being; man is made of corruptible matter.

An angel has most immediate dealings with God; he is the familiar of the Most High, as it were, His assistant. Man is like a stranger, by sin an exile far from God.

An angel is man's superior through the full splendor of divine grace; he shares abundantly in the beatific vision. True, man has his share in the light of grace, but so small is that share that he may be said to be walking in the dark.

---

[1] St. Bernard: *Missus est*, 3.

Therefore, that an angel should show reverence and deliver a Salutation to a human being was unheard of, until you, Gabriel, greeted the Blessed Virgin with your *Ave.*

That incomparable, matchless being is superior to an angel in every way. You yourself, one of the seven who in heaven keep their gaze fixed on the Godhead, wish to acknowledge that superiority.

That wish, good angel, makes you say: "Hail! I recognize that your share of grace is more abundant than mine, than ours, who are God's angels. I reverence you, because you excel me, you excel us, you excel every creature.

"You excel us, Mary, in familiarity with God, the Lord, who is with you; for in you He dwells as true Son of the Father; with us He is but Lord.

"You excel us in the purity of the light and splendor of spiritual beauty; you in yourself are the all pure way; you obtain that purity for others.

"That is why I, why we, we angels of heaven, are but your subjects, your servants, desiring only to be and to remain at your feet to carry out all your commands, even as we perform the will of God.

"That is why, Mary, I say to you: *Hail! full of grace, the Lord is with thee; blessed art thou among women.*"

Speaking thus in tones sweet and tender,[2] the archangel Gabriel—Mary's guardian angel, some believe—kept his head bowed in an attitude of utmost respect,[3] and with him the whole angelic court.

Tarry a little, Christian soul, before her whom heaven, through a spirit who is but the voice of the Most High, proclaims the Virgin of virgins, Mother of God, and your Mother.

---

2 St. Andrew of Crete: *Sermo in Annuntiatione.*
3 St. Bonaventure: *Meditatio vitae Christi,* c. IV.

3. THE VIRGIN IS TROUBLED

O Virgin Mary, what were you doing, while your archangel, resplendent in grace and glory, was delivering that Salutation? In what unbroken silence was your soul engulfed?

Assuredly, you were in prayer to God, praying to the Father in secret.[4] Gabriel assists at your prayer, as angels vie to do, and offers it to God in sweet-smelling sacrifice and holy devotion.

Your immaculate soul sinks into the bosom of the adorable Trinity, Father, Son and Holy Spirit. Most certainly your mind dwells on the ineffable Word about to come to earth to fulfill the promises of the centuries long gone.

Eternally predestined Daughter of the Triune God, you are not unaware of His designs upon you. You meditate on them, abasing yourself in that humility which attracts to you heaven and earth.

In your prayer's impressive silence you hear the cries of the afflicted, begging you for consolation. Their eyes fixed on you, their endless tears implore you.

From every corner of the universe gaping mouths cry to you for mercy. Those cries reach you from limbo, from earth, even from heaven; cries, tears, sighs, expression of their hearts' desires.

You hear the cry of Adam, your first father, the cries of all the patriarchs, of your forebears—all the kings of old—the cries of all the children of men, desolate, because heaven's gate is closed to them. You hold the key.

"And Mary," says the Evangelist, "was troubled... and thought with herself what manner of salutation this should be."[5]

You are troubled, Mary. Yet, you are unafraid. What is it that troubles you? Allow me in all humility to question you. Everything that happens to you is full of mystery—mystery and sanctity.

Is it the archangel that troubles you? Does his form, his beauty,

---

4 St. Matt. 6:6.   5 St. Luke 1:29.

the unfading youthfulness of his features distract you a moment from that pure prayer which lifts you up in ecstasy?

The mere thought would seem an affront, an insult! An immaculate Virgin conceived without sin, minus sin's imperfections and consequences—is she not absolute mistress of her emotions?

For long, aye at all times, angels have visited you, doubtless your guardian angel in particular. Could Satan ever transform himself into an angel of light before you, Virgin most prudent?

It is the very words of the Salutation that trouble you. Their content is so bewildering, so marvelous, so sublime, yes, something altogether divine.

But, a knowledge divinely infused, a knowledge that has continued and increased indefinitely, reveals to you that content.

That knowledge, in proportion to your graces, has of necessity expanded your supernatural forces; it gives your prudence and wisdom unequalled powers, and those powers a brightness which is a plenitude of light.

Much better than Gabriel, infinitely better than anyone can ever say, you know all that that Salutation contains. You are not unaware, Mary, that it contains the whole burden of your mystery.

You accept its message. God, through His archangel, once again confirms on earth that which from the beginning, from the day of your predestination, was conceived in His unchangeable thought.

It is because of your incomparable humility that you start and seem to be troubled. For that virtue, accustomed to instil into a soul a low opinion of self, finds it ever hard to believe what exceeds its expectations.

You do not doubt. You, whom God "has possessed in the beginning of his ways,"[6] will never doubt. But this reminder from heaven seems so lofty, so far beyond belief, that you feel overwhelmed.

---

6 Prov. 8:22.

Gabriel, an archangel, salutes you, calls you "full of grace," assures you that the Lord is with you as with no one else. He places you above every creature, you, the first of all, blessed among all women.

How overwhelming! The divine messenger understands clearly. All that he must still say to you in this, the most solemn moment of the world's history, will be the crowning blow to your humility.

His wish is to explain to you, as no one down the ages ever can, those few words: *Hail! full of grace, the Lord is with thee; blessed art thou among women.* Who does not understand that you need to be reassured and sustained lest you totter and collapse?

Fear not, Mary! [7] Till now Gabriel had not dared to pronounce that name—*Mary*—the name above every name except that of Jesus Christ. Who, then, even though an archangel, can utter it in fitting tones?

Mary! That name cannot be translated, so sublime is it, so many mysteries, so many oceans of knowledge and love does it embrace!

That name stands for fulness of grace, the presence of the Lord, blessedness unparalleled. To utter *Mary*... only He can who dowers that name with benediction beyond measure, that is, God Himself.

Mary! Immediately on hearing her name, the troubled Virgin becomes calm, regains her poise. That name which God uttered in eternity, in the bosom of the Three, has the singular power to reassure her who bears it.

Fear not, Mary. You have truly found grace with God. Do you look for proof? You will conceive in your womb and bear a Son to whom you will give the name, *Jesus.*

Behold! another way, a more complete and more exact, a more enlightening and more revealing way of saying: *Hail! full of grace,*

---

7 St. Luke 1:30.

the Lord is with thee; blessed art thou among women.

Full of grace! What unique grace you have found with God! Grace without parallel, grace never even dreamed of in ages gone by, the wonder of the universe; grace beyond all praise, excelling every grace of angels and men.

You have found the Son of God, a Son who has no mother in heaven and who finds one in you; a Son who will be called Jesus, because He will save His people and deliver them from their sins.

The Lord is with thee. Who, we ask, can be with you as much as He who will be your Son? as He who will be great, so great that He will be the Son of the Most High, of whose "greatness there is no end?"[8]

The Lord, His Father, will seat Him, King, on the throne of David, that throne of wisdom, the throne eternal, never to be overturned. On that throne He will reign without end, the Son whom you helped to place thereon.

How great He will be, that Lord, your Jesus and ours! Great in merit, power, dignity, in wisdom without peer, in holiness divine, in beauty beyond compare!

Of a truth He will be the Son of the Most High, He whose Mother you will be; for He is Himself the Most High, equal to the Father in all things.[9] *Blessed art thou among women!*

All of that will He be. But He is all that from eternity. Can He be any greater? Yes, because He who, being God, is already great, will be great also for having become Man.

Yes, He will be great, that Man-God. God will so raise Him up in glory before the mighty of this world, that peoples and kings will adore and serve Him.

But only in your bosom, in your arms will they adore Him, Mary, Virgin of virgins, Mother of God, Mother of angels and Mother of men, Mother of mankind in you reborn.

Oh! the constancy of your faith, Woman most blessed! Only too well you know that God in His own good time can accom-

---

8 Ps. 144:3.   9 Phil. 2:6.

plish all. You believe it, you accept it, because you rest that faith on the solid foundation of your humility.

4. THE BLESSED OF THE HOLY SPIRIT

Your incomparable humility, Mary, is now reassured. Such reassurance fortifies you and prepares you to hear whatever the Salutation suggests. I, too, would listen.

The *Hail Mary* serves to form that virtue in us. It is a matter of note that those devoted to that prayer, if they are not humble, become so and tirelessly grow in humility.

What that prayer contains and says is in fact so sublime that the soul meditating on it is swept along with you, Mary, to that emptying of self proper to every approach to its God. *He hath regarded the humility.*[10]

Humility is the foundation of another virtue—purity of heart in its every degree. It contains, Immaculate Virgin, the deep root of all virginity, above all, of yours.

I am not at all surprised that for another reason your response to the archangel's message was: *How shall this be done, because I know not man?* All my being is vowed to God alone.

To be sure, you do not doubt. You do not ask whether it is possible or not for a virgin to become the Mother of God; but only how, by what means, in what way this shall be done: *How shall this be done?*

At times we have read that, sooner than suffer any impairment of your virginity, you would renounce the extraordinary privilege of that maternity. But, no! you are wholly bound over to the manifest will of God.

True, you have made a vow; you have sworn to be His only. Not to keep that vow would naturally disturb you. Oh! may He, who wills to come to earth, accomplish the same in my regard!

---

10 St. Luke 1:48.

He can allow a virgin to conceive and bear a son, for to Him nothing is impossible. Would not that be solemn proof that He has regarded the lowliness of His handmaid? But how accomplish it?

Blessed art thou among women. Behold, Mary, the wonder of wonders! Gabriel has told you: "The Holy Spirit shall come upon thee, and the power of the Most High shall overshadow thee."[11]

What does he say? Are you not already filled with the Spirit of the Father and the Son? Can you be full of grace and still not have within you that same Spirit, the dispenser of all graces?

If He is already within you—and we know that He is within you with the fulness of singular grace—why does the angel promise that He will come upon you again? What does the angel mean?

The Holy Spirit will come upon you, on you who are full of grace. You will receive another grace, another fulness adding mysteriously to your first fulness.

That first fulness was chiefly for your soul. The fulness of the divinity, which dwells in you spiritually, as in many another saint, will begin to dwell in you corporally, in your virginal womb.

The power of the Most High shall overshadow thee. Let him who will, comprehend! O mystery of mysteries! Mystery that she alone can understand to whom alone was given the supreme happiness of experiencing it!

Can you reveal to us, Mary, how that inaccessible Splendor, the Spirit of the Father and the Son, stole into your chaste womb? how you were able to bear up under its divine approaches?

The Blessed Trinity alone brought to pass with you and in you alone the mystery hidden from the ages and generations,[12] the great mystery of mercy.[13] You alone deserved to understand it and above all to experience it.

The Holy Spirit would come upon you by His omnipotence;

---

11 St. Luke 1:35.   12 Col. 1:26.   13 1 Tim. 3:16.

He would render you fruitful. But His operation would be so veiled, so hidden in the impenetrable shadow of His secret designs that you and your Jesus alone would feel its effects.

How shall this be done? Do not ask Gabriel. You will know from Him who must accomplish it and show you how. The archangel is not commissioned to cause your virginal conception; he is charged only with announcing it to you.

Not by man's cooperation, but by that of the Spirit of Love will you conceive. That is why *By the very power of the Most High thou shalt conceive the true Son of God.*

For *the Holy which shall be born of thee shall be called the Son of God!*[14] No longer will He be only the One who descends from the Father's bosom into yours, but the One who borrows from your very own substance to become your very own son.

Just as He who was begotten of the Father from eternity is called His Son, so will He be called your son. And as He who is begotten of the Father is your son, He who is to be born of you will be His Son.

Not for that reason are there two sons, one the Father's, the other yours; there never will be but one Son. You will not each have your own, but He will be the Son of both. Oh! wonder of wonders!

The Holy which shall be born of thee... With what reverence the angel utters those words! He seems, Mary, to lack a suitable name to designate *the blessed fruit of thy womb,* as your cousin Elizabeth will soon describe Him.

The Father's only Son, that wondrous fruit, which will be formed from the union of soul and body, and which will be drawn from your pure body, how shall he name Him? Is there in heaven or on earth a name sublime enough to designate Him?

He does not find one. He says not the holy Flesh, or the holy Man, or the holy Child, or any such; none of those will suffice. He says: the Holy, a vague expression, the Holy, the Holy of

---

14 St. Luke 1:35.

Holies, that divine offspring conceived of the Holy Spirit.

Yes, with that fruit you will then be truly *full of grace,* of grace created and uncreated. You will have found it, discovered it again, recovered it through God's power for all mankind. You will be the Mother of Him who saves all who hope in Him.

What further, then, is needed to convince you? Need Gabriel announce to you that your cousin, Elizabeth, the barren one, has conceived a son? No! you are not in doubt. Will not Elizabeth soon praise you because you have believed?[15]

Nevertheless, the archangel tells you that, in order to crown your happiness of mother-elect; after intimating the first miracle, he discloses to you that second amazing miracle: a barren one who has conceived!

Heaven alone must needs announce that other grace to you before anyone else. The time will come when everyone will know that from the beginning of those mysteries, as varied as they are astonishing, you had full knowledge of them.

No, Mary, no word shall be impossible with God. Gabriel did not say: *Nothing is impossible,* but: *No word shall be impossible with God.*[16] In other words, with God alone is there no difference between doing and saying, between saying and willing.

With Him, who is Truth itself, the intention is the word. With Him, who is Power itself, the word is the act. With Him, who is Wisdom itself, the manner is the same as the act.

With heaven and earth attending, the archangel, bent in adoration above that virginal womb in which the eternal Word is about to become flesh, obtained the consent of the *blessed among women.*

She in turn, some revelations say, belittling herself in that humility which is so closely allied to grace, sank to her knees in profound adoration and, folding her hands, said to God whom she adored:

Behold the handmaid of the Lord; be it done to me according

---

15 cf. St. Luke 1:45.   16 St. Luke 1:37.

to Thy word.[17]

May the Word, who is in God from the beginning, become flesh of my flesh according to Thy word; may a virgin, with child through Thy Spirit, become the very Mother of God!

Mary was praying for herself and for the whole world ... God desires us to beg of Him in prayer the very things which He has promised and wishes to grant.

Be it done to me! a Word that my eyes can behold, that my arms can embrace, my kisses inflame with their tenderness, a Word of living flesh.

Be it done to me! such as has never before been done and never will be done hereafter to anyone! May He come down silently to me, a person in the flesh, a body in my womb!

Be it done to me! that Word who neither can begin to be or has need of beginning, the eternal One; grant me the grace that He be born of me for generation unto generation! Amen!

On the instant the Son of God, God and Man, was conceived whole and entire in the Virgin's womb. There He took flesh, whole and entire, while He still remained in His Father's bosom.

There, in the Ark of the Covenant He, who was in the form of God and who can always without robbery claim the homage due to God, emptied Himself by taking our form, the form of a servant.[18]

Perfect God that He is, He is born a perfect man, with a soul and body and all its different members. What shall I say? The new Adam, the new adorable head of a new race of new men whom He restores to life. There with Him we, too, are mystically conceived.

There in the womb of a Virgin-Mother we are reborn, you and I, mystically, to be sure, but really; so much so that she who becomes God's Mother at the same time becomes the Mother of men. The Mystical Body of Christ is one; the Head is and always will be inseparable from us, its members.

---

17 St. Luke 1:38.   18 Phil. 2:7.

With the archangel, with the heavenly choirs, with the ages lost in wonder and inflamed with love, Mary, on her knees, adores. For the first time the *Hail Mary* is uttered by men who since repeat:

Holy Mary, Mother of God, pray for us sinners, now and at the hour of our death. Amen. And Mary, greatly moved, adopted us as her children.

Holy Mary, Mother of God. The well known prayer epitomizes in a few words all the points on which we are meditating—Gabriel's Salutation and the Prayer that will be said over and over to the end of the world.

We can believe that at the very moment of His conception in the recess of the virginal womb the Incarnate Word offered to His Father the first act of adoration, the act of a Man-God, an act which by its infinite value could have satisfied every demand of that Father's glory.

He, the Eternal Priest, even then began to offer to His Father acts of perfect thanksgiving, of exceptional atonement, of efficacious supplication. All those acts began to rise from the Immaculate Heart of Mary as from an altar to atone signally for all the sins of men.

Next, He must needs direct His attention to her whom He had chosen as His Mother and at the same time as the Mediatrix and Dispenser of all grace, and, as St. Bernard calls her, the channel of His Mystical Body.

At that moment, doubtless, in the womb of her whom by a name so beautiful, so revered and so endearing we shall call Our Lady, He was the very first to bid her *Hail,* the Salutation of a God made Man.

There, too, a child of Mary should with perfect faith, invincible hope and ever-burning love bid her *Hail;* yes, there in her womb, where that Salutation re-echoed on the day of Our Lady's Annunciation.

O Mary, lowly in spirit and virginal in body, at the moment

when you manifested to God that faith, that hope and that love, you merited for us that Salutation.

Place on our lips and above all in our hearts, and keep it there unwearyingly, that Salutation which wins eternal salvation for us poor sinners!

May we spend our lives in saying: *Hail! Hail!* and again and again *Hail!* May it be our last sigh at the supreme hour, in the midst of our agony, in the smile of peace which you promise us at that moment! Amen.

PART ONE: THE ANGELIC SALUTATION

HAIL, MARY! FULL OF GRACE,
THE LORD IS WITH THEE;
BLESSED ART THOU AMONG WOMEN
AND BLESSED IS THE FRUIT
OF THY WOMB, JESUS.

CHAPTER I. AVE ... HAIL

GLORY OF THE AVE

AVE.... *Hail....*
That angelic salutation comes down from heaven, from God's heaven.

It re-echoes down the ages.
It re-echoed in the bosom of the Blessed Trinity—of the Father, Son and Holy Spirit, *ab initio et ante saecula*... before the beginning of things...

For, before the beginning of things,
before the light, the life, and the motion of all that is or moves,
Mary was saluted by the Holy of Holies.
The Father saluted His eternal Daughter;
the Son, His admirable Mother;
the Holy Spirit, His immaculate Spouse.
The Blessed Trinity as One salutes her ever and pauses before her matchless beauty, proclaiming her the All Beautiful, in whom there is no stain.

Ave... Hail...
An archangel, the archangel Gabriel, one of the seven who stand before God's Face,
he whose name signifies the Might of God,
he it is who brings that *Ave,* that *Hail,* to earth.
Let us say it again .... never before had an angel bowed to human creature.

But in that Virgin's presence he minimizes his greatness;
he knows that he is in the presence of his sovereign,
of the Queen of all the angelic hierarchies.
He is not alone. He is attended by thousands of those spirits,
by all the incomparable hierarchies.

Ave... Hail...
He intones the Salutation that God repeats over the endless ages in His eternal Mystery.
And all those magnificent hosts repeat, *Ave... Hail...*

Ave... Hail...
Behold!
the canticle of all the saints of God;
passionate song mingled with unparalleled admiration;
exaltation of prophets, apostles, martyrs;
tireless hymn of confessors, virgins, widows;
consolation of the humble and the lowly;
refuge of sinners;
strength of the sick;
rest for the weary;
prayer of great souls;
supplication of every man and woman who needs God.

Ave... Hail...
Behold!
the cry of my poor soul;
my sigh in distress;
my light in darkness;
my joy in sorrow;
my peace amidst care and anguish;
my safeguard in time of temptation.

Ave... Hail...
Virgin all beautiful;
Chosen and forechosen Vessel of God;

Greatest Wonder of the universe;
Barque of the entire world;
Paradise of delights, of concord, of immortality;
Tree of life, of joy and rapture;
Treasury of the faithful, and salvation of the world;
Glorious Throne of the Creator;
Most excellent Mediatrix between God and man;
Most efficacious Conciliatrix of the whole world!

Ave... Hail...
O Mary, hours, days, years would not suffice to unfold the meaning of that *Ave...* that *Hail*. To you, whom heaven and earth proclaim
> the sure salvation of all who with upright and sincere heart have recourse to you,
> *Ave, Ave, Ave... Maria!*
> *Hail, Hail, Hail... Mary!*

CHAPTER II. MARY
THE NAME ALL BEAUTIFUL

Hail, *Mary!*
A person's name always summons up his image.
I may never have met or seen him,
I know only the name he bears;
and lo! each time I utter his name,
he appears before my mind's eye. I see him, touch him,
speak to him, I bring him to life before me.
If it be the name of one I love, I feel in my heart a stirring of joy and comfort.
At the same time that name brings before me his virtues, his talents, his merits, his brilliant exploits.
Merit and glory attend that name.
To repeat it is to spread its fame, to carry that fame to every shore, to imprint it on every mind.
Names that are sacred and revered above all others we utter only with sovereign respect,
like a mystery that we cannot fathom,
a mystery from which in olden times the people dared not draw the veil of the sanctuary.
Israel considered the sacrosanct name of Yahweh superior to the whole Law.
Such are the names of Jesus and Mary.
In them we see the epitome of the New Law,

the treasury of the great wonders of religion,
and of the most sublime truths of the Gospel.

Hail, Mary!
When I utter those words, I breathe her name who is virgin and mother,
Mother of God and Mother of men, Mother of mine!
and behold! in an instant she is there before me.

I need not see her appear, as she did to so many others; I am too unworthy of that.

But when I say: *Mary!...* she is there. I am sure she is there, that she sees me, smiles on me, listens to me, stretches her arms out to me.

Mary!
Neither heaven nor earth can utter a name by which my faith and love receive more abundant grace,
I conceive a more assuring hope,
I experience a sweetness more divine.

Hail, Mary!
That name, a thousand times blessed, signifies a world of things. It is impossible for me or for anyone to enumerate them.

Recall that mystery at the world's beginning:
The Spirit of God moved over the waters,
not like a ship with sails spread flying before the wind and impelled by a favorable breeze,
but as a dove broods on its eggs to hatch them with its warmth. That vast expanse of waters Holy Scripture calls: *Maria,*[1] the seas.

Oh! well I know that in this case *Mary* and *Maria* are different names, with quite different meanings;
but a similarity of sound and of meaning, too, inspired God's

---

1 *Mária* is the plural of the Latin word, *mare*, meaning sea. *María* is a proper name, meaning Mary.

saints. The Holy Spirit, they say, quickens both and makes them both fruitful.

From the waters ... *Maria* ... of holy baptism come forth the adopted children of God;
> from *Mary* was born the true Son of God, the One who makes her the true Mother of God.

> *Hail, Mary!*
> That name most beautiful, most beautiful of all names,
> the richest, most fruitful, most mighty,
> after the holy Name of Jesus the most holy name.
> That name signifies all that we can conceive of the great, the sublime, in heaven and on earth.
> Alas! it is so godlike that it defies comprehension.
> When I say: *Mary,* I feel that I express something utterly transcendent.

Almost everywhere we read—and it is true—that that name signifies *Sovereign* and *Queen.*
> You rule, *Mary,* in heaven and on earth, and even in hell.
> You are the absolute Sovereign and Queen of all your Son's kingdom.
> In heaven all your subjects are crowned in the kingdom of the King of kings, in the paradise of God.
> Here on earth kings lay at your feet their diadems, their crowns, their very selves.

Hell is forced to bear the weight of your lasting hatred. Satan is more humiliated at seeing himself under the heel of the lowliest of creatures than at feeling himself crushed by God's almighty arm.

> You are my Sovereign and my very Queen.

That complete dominion over me, over my body, my soul, my senses, over all that I am and have,
> I desire it, I long for it, I am proud of it.

I salute that dominion as a shining star illumining and guiding my life.
I fix my gaze on that star and turn from it never.
I find faith in its light, hope in its help; I love it to distraction, as a slave of love, voluntarily delivered to the service of his great lady.

Hail, Mary!
O my soul, call on Mary, find comfort in her holy name!
Whisper that name without ceasing night and day.
Spell it out like a child.
Mary! Mary!
I know only how to lisp those two syllables: *Mary*.
But a mother, as she hears her child lisping his inarticulate pleas, is enraptured beyond all telling.
At all times, and better than she, you, you will understand me each time I repeat
Hail, Mary!

CHAPTER III. FULL OF GRACE

1. HER BEAUTY

Hail, *Mary, full of grace.*
    Nature has made you her masterpiece.
    I gaze on you here before me and I glow in your beauty's reflection.
    For, grace is poured abroad in thy lips,[1] *Mary.*
You are beautiful, yes, of creatures the most beautiful, the *all beautiful,*
    the one in whom there is no spot.[2]
    I speak not now of natural beauty only.
Full of grace, the Lord's free gift pours out from you, overflows from you, realizing in you the soul's every perfection,
    and all beauty of body.

    Your soul! what a storehouse of the ideal and the real!
    Jesus is the most beautiful of men;
    you were His mould, His mirror, and He yours.
A soul like yours, which must sustain all the marvels of grace, must itself be a marvel of nature.
    Therein we behold perfection of all its powers,
    depth and sureness of understanding, strength and tenacity of will,
    incomparable harmony of the lower faculties.
    It is the realm of peace.

---

[1] Ps. 44:3.   [2] Cant. 4:7.

Full of grace...
Your body, *Mary*, is the masterpiece of the power, wisdom and love of Him who was to become flesh of your flesh.
An immaculate soul like yours must needs be joined to incorruptible flesh, whose every perfection and all its superior splendor make for beauty.
In shaping your body God had in mind Jesus Christ; He labored but for Him.[3]
That body was destined to be the mould in which the Father's Word was to be cast, to become the Word Incarnate.
You were all beautiful, beautiful in mind, in body, in countenance, *tota pulchra,*
> with the charm of the purest of virgins,
> the majesty of the noblest of mothers,
> in integrity most perfect, in fruitfulness unequalled.
> Beautiful wherever you appear:
> at your presentation in the temple;
> in ecstasy before Gabriel as he gazed into your eyes;
> in Nazareth's hidden life in the light from Jesus' face;
> on the roads of Galilee and Judea, as you followed Jesus and listened to Him enraptured;
> at the foot of the holy Cross, and with Jesus dying;
> in the supper room beneath the fiery tongues of the Holy Spirit;
> ever in the glory in which with Jesus you reign.

Full of grace...
Eternity will not suffice, *Mary,* to contemplate the beauty which I behold in you.
To say that I shall one day behold—at least that is my hope—the beauty of your body and better still of your soul!
They say that a single soul in the state of grace by far excels in beauty all other earthly beauty—beauty of flowers, of the

---

[3] Bossuet: *1 sermon sur la nativité de la Sainte Vierge.*

firmament, of all nature.
Because you are immaculate, your beauty, we may say, surpasses infinitely that of all souls in the state of grace.
Souls themselves excel one the other to a degree as yet unknown. What must be the beauty of the hundredth, more beautiful as it is than the ninety-nine others?
And the thousandth... the hundred thousandth?
This last possesses one hundred, one thousand, one hundred thousand times more beauty than the first.
I picture the most beautiful of all. What is its beauty compared to yours?
Scarcely beauty's shadow!

If one were to behold the beauty of a single Angel, of even the least of the Angels, he would be apt to mistake him for God and adore him.
Now, the least among the Archangels surpasses beyond compare the most beautiful Angel.
And the least of the heavenly Virtues surpasses the greatest of the Archangels.
I continue upwards to the Principalities, to the Dominations, to the Powers, to the midst of the Thrones, grading in like manner the beauty of each of those angelic Orders.
Comparing ever, I reach the Cherubim of Glory, and higher still the Seraphim burning with love.
Each of those hierarchies, the higher its rank, becomes more numerous than its predecessor.
Those spirits are myriad, says Holy Scripture.
What, tell me, must be the beauty, the splendor, the indescribable sublimity of the greatest, the highest of the Seraphim!
Yet, even among those, there is nothing to match your beauty, Virgin most beautiful!
They are merely God's servitors; you, you alone are His Mother. Is not that enough?
One who beheld your beauty, the little saint of Lourdes, could

declare: "I would be willing to die, could I behold it once more."

O Mary, full of grace, hail!
I am speechless, bewildered by the charm of your beauty.
Yet, I have still greater things to say.

2. SANCTIFYING GRACE

Hail, Mary! full of grace...
Nature has lavished on you all possible beauty.
But what is all that compared to your store of supernatural beauty?
You are *full of grace,* the precious gift,
   which God bestows on the soul, the special object of His love;
   which endows the soul with beauty pre-eminent;
   which renders it so pleasing in His eyes,
   that in it He discovers countless charms;
   which gives it such refinement of beauty as to captivate Him.
   It is impossible for Him not to love it.

This is that sanctifying grace, which makes the soul possessing it holy, which lifts a soul to such a height that it is God's adopted child, and the lawful heir to His eternal kingdom;
   so much so that God Himself cannot disinherit it;
   for, the kingdom belongs to it by right,
      in so ample a share that God puts the soul in possession of His goods and of Himself forever.
What a store of riches in habitual sanctifying grace!

Full of grace...
That grace is neither matter, nor spirit, nor substance.
It is neither a portion of divinity, nor of the Person of the Holy Spirit, nor a new soul added to ours.
Some have averred each of the above, but have erred.

Grace is a supernatural gift, a spiritual quality, placed by God in the soul, a pouring out of His own very splendor.
Its action on the soul may be compared to the sun's light penetrating a crystal sphere, or to the action of fire heating iron and making it glow red hot.
Light is only a quality, not the substance of the sun;
heat is but a quality, not the substance of fire.
The sun does not give its substance to the crystal sphere, nor does fire give its substance to the iron which it makes red hot. Otherwise, the crystal sphere would be the sun, the iron would be fire.
Both give their qualities only.
Nevertheless, we may say that the sphere, exposed to the sun's light, becomes a sun.
We may say that the red hot iron in the furnace is truly converted into fire.
Thus, grace is a certain participation in God's nature, that nature which is above all nature.
God's prerogative it is, and His alone, who is Being itself, an ocean of infinite perfections, to bestow on a soul which He sanctifies by His habitual grace such a resemblance of Himself that He seems to endow that soul with His own very nature.

And yet, it is but a created participation of His nature. It is a splendor which envelops the soul, penetrates it, transforms it, which renders it deiform. It does not make it God, but very like unto God. If we could behold the beauty which that soul acquires through that grace, we would take that soul for God Himself.
In that soul God recognizes His child, the child which He adopts and to which He gives, through grace, what is His by nature.
No, that soul does not become God; it still remains a creature.
But God Himself, who, being altogether simple, contains an infinity of perfections with all their matchless beauty,

endows that soul with that sanctifying grace, which renders it so like to Him that we may say that that soul is invested with His own very nature.

And who gives this grace?
Oh marvel of love! In itself grace is only a creature like the soul for which it is destined.
However, Holy Scripture does not state that God draws it out of nothing.
It flows directly from the bosom of the Blessed Trinity, from the bosom of Love itself.
> "It is poured forth in our hearts, by the Holy Spirit, who is given to us."[4]

We may call it a precious liquid flowing from one vase to another. And, since the Holy Spirit is, in a sense, the Heart of the Father and the Son, that grace empties from their Heart into ours.
I am only a vile creature; still, my soul becomes divinized! In a very true sense it becomes like to God!
I think that were my soul to behold itself in possession of that sanctifying grace, and realize its value, it could scarcely survive a moment on earth. It would expire for very joy!

It was necessary to repeat all the above as a parenthesis in order to understand the praise we bestow on Mary, when we say to her:
> *Hail, Mary! full of grace.*

Full of that sanctifying grace which likens her to God as it does no other pure creature.
For, if any soul has been flooded with the spirit of grace and, as it were, deluged by the torrents of grace flowing from the Heart of God, it is, after that of the God-Man, her soul, hers alone.
Well might Gabriel say: *Thou hast found grace with God.*[5]
No one has found or received grace like Mary.

---

4 Rom. 5:5.   5 St. Luke 1:30.

3. THE IMMACULATE ONE

Hail, Mary! full of grace.
Thus you revealed yourself long ago to Bernadette at the grotto of Massabielle.
When she asked: "Who are you, beautiful Lady?"
You replied: *"I am the Immaculate Conception."*
No two things are more incompatible, more opposed, than God and sin.
God is infinite good; sin, infinite evil.
How can sin approach the throne of God?
The closer a soul is to God, the farther it is from sin.
But, no one, *Mary,* could have had a closer approach to God than you.
It is impossible for any creature to be closer to God's Son than His own Mother.

From eternity, before anything was, you were united to your Son, Jesus Christ, by indescribable bonds.
"The Lord possessed me in the beginning of his ways."[6]
For, when in eternity God decreed the incarnation of the Word, His very own Son, through you alone,
> you were conceived in His design, in the same plan as Jesus, from eternity.

Because all things are done for Him, for you also all things are accomplished.
The whole angelic creation, all human kind and every inferior thing, all is for Him, for you.
From eternity the future conception of the God-Man included that of His Mother.
Since the conception of the Son of God is all holy, all pure, infinitely removed from every appearance of sin,
> it is supremely fitting that the conception of her, from whom

---

6 Prov. 8:22.

He will one day be born, be equally far from sin.
For that reason, Virgin most pure, you were conceived by your mother, St. Anne, without even the shadow of sin.
Because of your eternal predestination to be the Mother of God, original sin, which like all Eve's daughters you should have contracted, could not touch you.
Such a stain would have reflected evermore upon your Son, Jesus, who is Holiness itself.
With what insolence Satan could have said: "I have overcome Thee in Thy Mother. She who gave Thee life was at least for an instant wholly in my power."
But, no! Not so!
You are so sinless, Mary, that you can declare:
I am the Immaculate Conception.
I make, above all, an act of faith, when I cry:
Hail, Mary! full of grace.
In you sin cannot be thought of.
In you there is only God's grace.
In you only His splendor, His light, His love, His unspeakable delight.
You are truly His beloved Daughter, the only one in whom there is no stain.
With you all is pure, virginal, immaculate.
You were conceived, you were born "Lily of the glorious and ever peaceful Trinity."
In you there is no remainder of concupiscence with its bitter consequences.
You are God's holiest creature, the one destined to conceive and bear the Holy of Holies;
> the one who conceives in your womb along with Him the multitude of God's holy men and women.

O full of grace, who would not honor and glorify you?
Who would not love you, you who are most beautiful, the one in whom there is no stain?

4. FULNESS OF GRACE

Hail, Mary! full of grace
You are, Mary, a torrent of graces, of those graces which make you the most blessed among women.
You are a spiritual ocean of grace.
Who can understand it?
The combined intellects of men and angels cannot conceive the spiritual fulness of your soul.
Who can imagine the storehouse of grace that God willed to use in building the living temple in which Infinite Wisdom would come to hold His court for nine months?
Think of it! from eternity God the Father begets His only Son.
But that same only Son, inasmuch as He is Man, the Man-God, Mary conceives in time.
Behold! the Father and Mother of the same divine Person!
No more than the Father does Mary engender the divine nature.
That is of itself.
Just as the Father really begets the divine Person of His Son, so Mary really conceives the divine Person of that same Son, in so far as He is incarnate.
> For the Father, begetting is a necessity,
> for the Mother, conceiving is a miracle;
> to both, glory forever!

O Mary, how is that miracle, exclusively yours, accomplished?
From your very own substance you conceive that Word, in you made flesh, your only Son.
Your substance is not superabundant, as is the Father's;
> remaining a created substance, it does not possess His infinite perfections.

What gives you the power to conceive a Man-God from your own substance?
An unheard-of grace of necessity supplies what is wanting in your nature.

Where do you find that grace?
You exhaust God's treasures, although they are inexhaustible.
For, I repeat, you have found that grace.
However, even then, even after exhausting those treasures, you will always remain a creature; you will not be God, as is the Father of your only Son.
Shall I say that in order to be equally the Mother of the Eternal Word, you must needs be equal to God?
God forbid! Who would dare so to blaspheme?
But I cite St. Bernardine of Siena, one of your most illustrious servants:
> "Mary should of necessity have been elevated to a certain equality with God."

He did not say to a perfect, but to a certain equality with God.
In comparison with God, Mary is nothing.
But may I not compare the copy with the original?
Did not God create man to His image and likeness?
Mary should of necessity have been elevated to a certain equality with God.
Thus is vindicated God's supreme glory in His unequalled greatness. Thus also does Mary's glory attain the peak to which the noblest of creatures can arrive.

From all this I draw another conclusion which captivates my soul. If all the above is true, Mary—and I am ready to die in defense of it—you received a greater store of grace than all other creatures together.
Your fulness of grace is such that it exceeds the countless number of graces granted to the nine choirs of angels,
>   to all the saints in heaven, on earth and in purgatory,
>   to all who will be to the end of time.

You are more replete with grace than all paradise itself.
For, all the combined graces of angels, saints, and all men present, past and future could not elevate them to so great an equality

with God as to produce, as you did, His only Son.
None of those can even conceive the kind of endless chain of graces which is yours.
But is that too much for the Mother of God?
For that you, and you alone, are worthy of more homage than all the angels and saints together.
We, too, for that reason, feel obliged to render you more honor, praise and reverence than we show to all the angels and saints. The latter we honor with a veneration called dulia;
> but for you, and you alone, we reserve a higher veneration, hyperdulia.

Can we do aught but imitate God Himself?

> *Full of grace...*

When we reflect with the most renowned theologians on the reason for her predestination to the divine motherhood,
> and for her Immaculate Conception which such a predestination required,
> we realize that from the first moment of her conception in the womb of her mother, St. Anne, Mary possessed the grace which we have contemplated in her,
> a grace that from the first instant already excelled that of the nine angelic hierarchies,
> that of all God's saints, and of all men, past, present and to be.

When we consider that that initial grace was the first of an endless chain of graces becoming always more numerous, more profound, more efficacious, more sublime, more Godlike,
> until at the hour of her blessed dormition in the evening of life it reached its final fulness, we are bewildered, speechless, lost in ecstasy.

We begin to understand something of the versicle of her *Magnificat:*
> "He who is mighty hath done great things to me."

5. MEDIATRIX

Hail, Mary! full of grace...
For your own sake, Mary, you are filled with divine life.
But, as Mother of mankind, as Mother of the living prefigured in Eve, whom in every way you excel,
    for us you are a superabundance of grace.
According to God's will in His eternal plan, you were wondrously the associate of Jesus in everything, because you gave Him birth. Now, that same Jesus wishes you to give Him birth anew in our souls, in wretched me.
He wills that, as you were the Mother of His natural body, you be Mother of His Mystical Body.
No one can be born to God in Christ Jesus, without being born also in you.
That is why I and with me all my brethren in Jesus Christ need to be enriched from your fulness of grace.
Jesus and you are inseparable in the work of my salvation.
Your will united to His consents, concurs, operates, merits, satisfies, intercedes to obtain for us that grace, for each according to his needs.
So God has willed it, and He does not retract.

Oh! we know that Jesus is the principal cause of all salvation's effects;
    but in them you cooperate with Him.
    After Him, you are the model of the predestined.
In justice, by reason of His merits, He obtains the grace of salvation for us;
    you acquire it for us as fitting return for your close cooperation in that task.
    Jesus paid the whole price of our redemption;
    in your own way you cooperated in that redemption.
In heaven Jesus intercedes with His Father by displaying His sacred wounds;

you are the supplicating force.
Hence, we call you the Mediatrix of all grace.
Jesus remains our Mediator with the Father;
you are our Mediatrix with Jesus.
Who, better than you, can fill that office?
You are so good, so tender, so merciful!
No one can intercede like you!

Jesus possesses the absolute fulness of grace;
He exhausts all its possibilities.
He is a shoreless sea, embracing all the oceans of grace.
As Man-God He sounds the depths of grace, His divinity.
Who can be closer to God than He?
Considering God's ordinary power, His grace, as Man, is a plenitude without limit in the highest possible degree.

In another sense, Mary, that fulness is yours.
You possess His grace on deposit for us.
You are its appointed dispenser.
Jesus communicated to you all that He acquired by His life and death, His infinite merits, His admirable virtues.

You are the treasure-house of all that His Father gave Him as heritage.

Through you He applies His merits, communicates His virtues, and dispenses His graces to all the members of His Mystical Body. You are the secret channel, the clear-flowing conduit through which sweetly and abundantly He sends the stream of His mercy.[7] That is why St. Bernard declares that no grace comes down from heaven to earth without passing through your hands.

Hail, Mary! full of grace.
Through you God gave us Jesus Christ.
Through you alone He gives us Him anew for all time, wishing to make us partakers of His riches.

Ave, gratia plena! Hail, full of grace!

---

7 St. Grignon de Montfort.

CHAPTER IV. THE LORD IS WITH THEE

1. THE PREDESTINED ONE

T HE *Lord is with thee.*
O heavenly Gabriel, what a wondrous grace of the sovereign Lord you are announcing to Mary!
The Lord is with thee.
Tell us, do, in what way and to what extent He is with her, and she with Him.
That Lord!
The Lord of heaven and earth, Lord of every creature; in particular, Mary, your Lord.
The Lord most mighty, most wise, most rich, the Lord eternal.
Has anyone ever seen the like? Will anyone ever see the like again?
You are, holy Virgin, the noble Daughter, the stainless Mother, the immaculate Spouse of the Lord,
> of that Lord, One in Nature, in Persons three, and you His lowly handmaid.
> For certain, Mary, the Lord is with you.
> He always was, He always is, He always will be with you,
> as the sun with the dawn which it announces;
> as the flower with the bush which produces it;
> as the king with the queen who may rightfully approach him.

Jesus is the most brilliant of suns, the most precious of flowers, the King of kings!

And He is with you, and you with Him.
Who can tell your greatness?

The Lord is with thee.
I have already said it, but it is good to repeat it and to explore that mystery.
The Lord is with you from eternity, before the beginning of things, before anything was.
From eternity God nourishes a design magnificent and above all designs stupendous.
He plans the creation of a Man who will be God.
A Man-God, His own Son, His Thought, His Word, in whom His Thought is expressed fully.
In His eternal councils He plans Jesus, the Christ.
That Jesus, in His time, will be the greatest, the most splendid of His creations, infinitely excelling all others.
He will be the beginning, the middle and the end of all creation.
He will be its only Head. He will sum up in Himself all that is, all that moves, all that lives, in heaven and on earth.
He will be creation's perfect embodiment.
God wills it, in spite of Satan, who at the given hour will attempt by his sin and man's to upset that plan.
Now, to realize that plan, that unique masterpiece, God's goodness has at its disposal an infinity of means;
He decides on one only, the one of His eternal election and predestination.
You are that one, Mary!

He who is, and who was, and who is to come[1]... will be born of your virginal womb, of your most pure flesh and blood.
You will be in the true sense of the word the Mother of God.
And, because Mother of God, at the same time Mother of men.
The Lord Jesus and you; from then on you two will be inseparable. All things were created by Him, the Word who is the Lord;

---

1 Apoc. 1:8.

all things were created for Him,[2] the Incarnate Word, the Lord Jesus. Consequently, we may say that all creatures were made for you, too, Mary.
The vast and stable universe points to you, as to Him.
What is His by nature is fittingly yours by grace.
From that fittingness come all your privileges, all your prerogatives, all your joys, your sorrows, your glory.
You share in His universal mediation, that of angels and that of men;
> into your hands He will put all graces to be dispensed for the salvation of the elect.

As He is the immortal King of the ages, you will be the world's Queen.
The heavenly hierarchies, the generations of men will proclaim you blessed, their sovereign faithful and lowly.
> Their homage will be but a bondage of love.
> It will be their rapture, their joy.

For all that, I sing your praise, first among women, so worthy of Him who is first among men.
> To such an extent is the Lord with you.
> But, that is not all.

2. MAGNIFICAT

Mary! The Lord is with thee.
A saint calls you *the complement to the whole Trinity.*[3]
But, what can be lacking to a Being absolutely perfect?
To the Father, the Son or the Holy Spirit?
Why, that Being would not be God!
Neither Jesus, as Man, all holy as He is, nor you, Virgin most perfect, are necessary to God.
God is sufficient to Himself; He needs only Himself.

---

2 Col. 1:16.   3 St. Hesychius: *Patr. Constant.*

But, can He not, so to speak, increase outside of Himself, acquire greater glory, at least extrinsic glory, and by that very fact enhance in His creatures' eyes His Being's beauty?
Can He not unite with a creature, and that to such an extent that we must admit that He is with her as with no one else?

> *O Mary, the Lord is with thee.*

In that way, in His being with you, you add to, complete, bring to absolute perfection, if we may so speak, our great God.
Is not that, after all, the meaning of that wondrous word: *Magnificat?*

> "My soul," you said, "doth magnify the Lord; it rejoices in Him."

It is as if your very being enlarged still more the dimensions of the Incommensurable. *Magnificat anima mea Dominum!*
Who will ever sound the depths of that prayer, of that canticle?
Your saints and doctors, Virgin all beautiful, attempt it in vain; it is an unfathomable abyss.
God alone knows what He placed in it for you, O Woman, whom He possessed from the beginning of His ways.
I am not surprised that the Church does not omit that prayer, that canticle, on any one day of the year.
Not even on Good Friday!
Did not that day, too, magnify God?

> *The Lord is with thee.*

The Father of heaven is with you, as He is with no one else, since He permits you, Mary, to glorify Him, even though extrinsically. By His intelligence, by knowing Himself, Himself and all other things,
He conceives and begets His Son from eternity.
And that Son, heavenly Father, begotten of Your bosom, exhausts Your paternal fruitfulness.
He is Your only Son, consubstantial with You, God of God, true God of true God.

In that Your will and its freedom have no part.
Your Word is necessary.
Without Him, You would not be God, there would be no God.
He is begotten of the Father, He is His Father's Word, His Father's Thought;
He, the secret Word, is the expression of that Thought.
Infinite Word, which mirrors His Father totally! His Father and all His Father's Thoughts!
Word without voice, without syllables, without a succession of phrases, without commentary.
One only Word expresses in itself the infinite world of all possible thoughts;
> one only Word expresses in itself the infinite world of words that can be spoken;
> one only Word, the Son of God, manifests all God's glory, both the glory that is within God Himself,
> and that which is outside Him.

Now, that Word could externalize itself in some way, take a body and appear in visible form.
> A new Word ever ancient and unique,
> but the sensible divine expression of the Ineffable!

Yes, the Father freely willed that Word; He made Him and He is Jesus, the Christ.
> And for you, Mary, He made Him.
> Mother of the Word which never will be unspoken!
> From the time that Word issued from your womb, we have seen Life itself;
> we hear it, we touch it.
> Through you we hear that eternal Word spoken in time.
> What a glorification of the Son!

Could You not, heavenly Father, by a free act of Your will, produce Him again outside Yourself, without separating Him from Yourself? Would not that be, in a way, to increase and magnify Yourself? Not only can You do it, but You willed it ever in the

infinite ages of ages.
It was to realize that masterpiece of masterpieces that You chose to create *Mary*.
She will be the virginal instrument of that divine increase.
Magnificat! He who in the Blessed Trinity is called the Son of God, will be at the same time Mary's Son, born from her womb, overshadowed by the Spirit of the Father and the Son.
We all, angels and men, shall acknowledge Him, we shall adore Him, as the one and only Jesus Christ, our Lord.
Oh! that Son of God, magnified by the Son of Mary! *Magnificat!*
To such an extent did God the Father will to be with *Mary*.

> *The Lord is with thee.*

Virgin all beautiful, the Son of God, the Word of the Father, deems it His great glory to be with you.
That is how you can magnify, and, as it were, increase, God the Son. *Magnificat anima mea Dominum!*
He is begotten in the bosom of the Trinity, God of God, Light of Light.
Through Mary it will be given to the only Son, who is in the bosom of the Father, to manifest the Father to us;
> by the very fact that He is born of your womb, Mary ... *Magnificat!*
> To such an extent did the Son of God will to be with you!

> *The Lord is with thee.*

You may, Mary, increase and magnify the Holy Spirit, the Love of the Father and the Son ... *Magnificat!*
Spirit of the Father and the Son, You who are by procession the adorable fruit of both, will You remain sterile and not in Your turn produce a Person?
From Your substance, no! It is impossible, for You exhaust their mutual love.
But, the Virgin, can she not give You the means?
Through her You can become the principle of a new fruit, ever

ancient.
You can be the principle of a divine Person born, not of Your essence, but by Your power.
Be, then, the divine Spouse of the Immaculate One!
In Your shadow she will give birth to the Son of the Most High. Joseph, the Just One, who will guard that ineffable and secret union, will also be Your shadow.
He will be mistaken for the husband of that Virgin Mother and consequently father of Jesus in the strict sense of the word.
But the power of the Most High, the power that will make Mary, the virginal earth, fruitful, will be You, and You alone.

    You will be fruitful of Jesus, the Word of the Father,
    fruitful of the first-born among many brethren.[4]
    Thus, the Father's eternal Daughter, the Son's admirable Mother,
    will be called the Immaculate Spouse of the Holy Spirit. She will have magnified You ... *Magnificat!*
    To such an extent God the Holy Spirit will be with *Mary!*

    O glorious fruitfulness of the whole Blessed Trinity!
    O complete fulfilment of a God's designs through a Virgin!
    Magnificat!
Since the hour of your visit to St. Elizabeth, mother of St. John the Baptist, the ages have chanted it, they are chanting it now, they will chant it forever!
    Well did Gabriel declare:
    Hail, Mary! full of grace, the Lord is with thee.

3. THE FRUITFUL SPRING

Hail, Mary! with whom the Lord is, with whom He is in a very special way!

---

4 Rom. 8:29.

He is with you by His goodness.

"God by His essence is goodness itself," says St. Leo.

Now, good can do all things, one thing alone excepted; it cannot contain itself.

It must communicate, spread and diffuse itself in every possible way.

The greater it is, the less it can contain its outpouring.

If it did not find satisfaction in pouring out its abundance, it would not endure.

God, the Father, the Son and Holy Spirit by their essence are goodness itself.

From eternity the Father, infinite Good, must diffuse Himself in His Son without ceasing.

Being alike, identical in the Son, the goodness of the Father and of the Son must diffuse and communicate itself entirely to the Holy Spirit.

The Holy Spirit, still goodness itself, cannot, like the Father and the Son, communicate Himself to another divine Person;

but He communicates Himself to her who approaches nearest to the divine Persons.

He pours Himself out into you, Mary, the Virgin-Mother, the Spouse of the Love of the Father and the Son.

And you, who so admirably inherit that Good! He makes you fruitful in such a way that you give flesh to a divine Person in a human nature. And that makes you truly the Mother of God.

The Good in you, therefore, becomes the inexhaustible spring of an infinity of blessings which pour themselves out on the Church.

O marvel of infinite goodness!

Are you, perhaps, Mary, that spring which from the creation of the world God placed in the midst of the earthly paradise, in the Eden of delights?

The holy doctors, who sing your praises, have so declared

again and again.⁵

A wondrous thing! Unlike ordinary water, which flows downward,
the waters of that spring ascend upwards. *A spring rose out of the earth.*

It rose and spouted in towering streams from the bosom of the earth, to divide into four great rivers and water the face of the earth. "It watered the face of the earth."

It brought to all the land the freshness, the fruitfulness to produce everything that could serve to nourish living beings.

We know that that paradise was a type of the Church; but the spring, says St. Jerome, is you, O Virgin, foster-mother of all the elect.

Holy Scripture gives the names of those great rivers, each of which has its own meaning; at the same time they reveal in you the wonders of divine goodness.

Their names are: Phison, Gehon, Tigris, Euphrates.⁶

The first river is called Phison, which means that it produces gold. Gold must be bought, cost what it may. To possess it, says Wisdom, one must give his all.

    Gold is holy love, holy charity.

    It is sanctifying grace, of which Scripture speaks.

    Without that we perish forever.

What a mighty river! what streams reach out from it—the sacraments, and all the practices of our holy religion.

The river Phison, which contains more precious waters than all the gold which it carries down, is the abundance of sanctifying grace;

    it is Jesus Christ, the Son of God, the Son of *Mary.*

Jesus, the Man-God, is not such of Himself; He is such through His Father. Without the Father, what would He be?

As Man, He is such through His most holy Mother. Without her,

---

5 P. d'Argenton: *Confér. théol. sur la Ste. Vierge.*   6 Gen. 2: 11–14.

what would He be?
He receives all His divinity from the Father, all His humanity from His Mother.
To be the great river of grace which sanctifies and saves, He must be God and Man.

>To produce Him, Father and Mother exhaust their substance.
>The Father makes Him like Himself;
>the Mother makes Him like to us.
>Those two are the spring from which the river takes its rise.
>O adorable Father! O Mother most admirable!
>How the Father is with *Mary!* and how *Mary* is with the Father!
>And how the two are with Jesus!

The second river is called Gehon, which means the outpourings of the bosom, of the heart.

>As God, Jesus courses eternally from His Father's bosom, and from there descends into your bosom, Mary, to issue from it like to us,
>to give Himself to us, to open to us His Heart.
>From that Heart we draw all the treasures of eternity.
>From those bosoms, the eternal and the temporal, flows the great river of grace,
>to water the earth, whose face is the Church, its beauty matchless. "It watered the face of the earth."

Did He not on one occasion exclaim: "If any man thirst, let him come to me and drink?"[7]
We may drink of that divine river as we wish.
And ever, as from two springs, as from a double bosom which pours itself out, our thirst is quenched.

>One is the Father's eternal bosom;
>the other Mary's virginal bosom.
>Who will ever doubt that the Lord is with her, and she with Him?

---

7 St. John 7:37.

The name of the third river is Tigris, which means the flying arrow. What can they be, those flying arrows?
They are the actual graces, God's holy inspirations; the graces which prevent, impel, move our wills so often rebellious.
We may call them the arrows of love which pierce the heart to make it die to sin, to lead it to repentance.

    It is a river of mercy and pardon.
    The heart is so often sealed, so often drowsy, asleep!
    What can open our heart, arouse it and stir it lovingly to come to God?

Those arrows are sent flying by the great river, Jesus; arrows which turn over the sterile and ungrateful soil of our souls.
But, Mary holds the quiver; she hands the arrows to her divine Son, for Him to wound us with them.

I have read, holy Virgin, Dispenser of grace, that you have charge of those graces which we receive.
Since you carried Jesus, the eternal Word, in your bosom, you have a certain control of the temporal treasures of the Spirit of love.
I have read that no grace comes from heaven without passing through your hands.
Jesus is the source which directs the floods.
You are the channel through which the streams flow, to pour themselves into every part of the Mystical Body.

    The heavenly Father first directs them from His bosom into Jesus' soul,
    and from that soul they flow into the Virgin-Mother's soul.

Thus, it seems that you, Mary, in a way control the divine inspirations that flow into my soul.

    You are like an ocean of divinity.
    From you issue all the rivers and streams of grace;
    and the spring is your all-pure bosom.
    You have that control over all the gifts, all the virtues, all the

graces of the Holy Spirit.
By your hand God distributes them when and to whom and as much as He wills.
Could God be with you more?

There remains the fourth river, the Euphrates, which means abundance of fruit.
In the spiritual order, that river, with its luxuriant banks, possesses all fruit in abundance for time and eternity.
In it, Mary, I contemplate the merits of all the good works that were, that are, that ever will be performed by your servants.
In it I see
the labors of apostles,
the sufferings of martyrs,
the prayers of contemplatives,
the austerities and prolonged trials of confessors,
the heroic struggles of virgins,
the admirable constancy of widows,
the charity of the rich, the poor's patience;
in a word, all the fruits of the practical virtues of the Church.
Truly, you have become the true garden of the Lord, the new earthly paradise.
What shall we say of the countless fruits which holy men and women of God have already gathered and harvested and stored in the heavenly paradise of glory?
It was the Euphrates that produced them all.
The Euphrates, that is, He who is the Son of your holy virginity;
of your all-pure spring, most holy Mother of God!
God was with you, as with no one else, for you to produce such an abundance,
and to remain the center of all good things.

Yes, truly we repeat to satiety:
Hail, Mary! full of grace, the Lord is with thee.

CHAPTER V. BLESSED ART THOU AMONG WOMEN

Hail, *Mary! full of grace, the Lord is with thee; blessed art thou among women.*
This is the canticle of canticles, Mary, the holiest, most secret, most profound of all the canticles sung in your honor:
"There are threescore queens, and young maidens without number.
One is my dove," my Immaculate One,
"the only one... the chosen...
The daughters, the queens saw her and declared her blessed."[1]
In such figurative language the generations have acknowledged you and will acknowledge you forever.
There is only one Woman, the most excellent Woman we have ever known.
"Clothed with the sun, and the moon under her feet, and on her head a crown of twelve stars";[2]
the Woman resplendent with the fires of divinity which consume her with love;
possessing every virtue, which like stars of the firmament adorn and beautify her ever.
Woman of all women blessed, excelling all out of measure, how beautiful you are!
You are the most beautiful, the only one, the chosen one!
Only after her rejection was Eve, the first woman, called the

---

1 cf. Cant. 6:7–8.   2 Apoc. 12:1.

Mother of the living.[3]

Alas! how much she lost for us all by her sin! And yet we give her a title that belongs rightly to you, Mary ...

From that time on she became, she remained your best prophet and forerunner.

From then on she called out to you, the Woman who was to crush the head of the infernal serpent under your immaculate heel.

> A great saint calls the genealogy of Jesus Christ a heavenly ladder having many different rungs.
> On it he pictures two women, one at the top, the other at the bottom.
> One is the mother of death, the other the Mother of Life;
> one who was overcome by the devil, the other who vanquished and overcame him;
> one who poisoned her race, the other who prepared for it the remedy;
> one who brought a curse on all her descendants;
> the other who causes blessings to reach back to the very earliest of her forbears;
> who, besides, showers those blessings generously on all who come after her.[4]

All the saintly Fathers and Doctors join the Church, *Mary,* in singing your praise.

You changed the ancient curse to benediction ever new.

You repair what Eve spoiled.

> "Unhappy woman," Tertullian says of her,
> "You were the devil's conquest, the guide to the forbidden fruit, the first to break your Lord's command, to mislead Adam, whom the serpent dared not attack;
> you shattered the beautiful image of the Creator, in atonement for which a God was forced to die."[5]

---

3 Gen. 3:20.   4 St. Bruno: *Serm. de Nat. B.M.V.*
5 *De habitu mulierum,* c. 1.

"But, be comforted, poor creature," cries St. Bernard;
"the hour has come in which the shame which you have incurred will be removed.
No longer will it be permitted to tell Adam that the woman whom he received from God has enmeshed him in Satan's snares.
He will be forced to admit that by woman he has been freed.
Hasten, Eve, and stand before Mary!
Let the Daughter answer for the mother;
let her stay her Father's censure and reproach;
for, if in the fall man was ensnared by woman, by woman alone will he rise again;
but by a Woman full of prudence, who replaces the foolish, imprudent one;
by a humble Woman, who is given him in place of a proud one;
by a Woman, who gives him life, instead of one who brings him death."[6]

Come, then, all ye women, of whatever condition!
come and render homage to her who restores your honor!
Come, ye virgins, pay respect to her who is your model and your queen!
come, ye mothers, and greet her who is your greatest glory!
come, ye young mothers, come and venerate, admire, sing the praise of the most chaste young mother of all!
Let every age, every state, every profession,
let all men come and proffer the same reverence to her who by the Blessed Fruit of her womb saves them!
Let both men and women strive to serve, to love, to thank Mary, the blessed among women!
For, through her alone, chosen as she was from among women, Jesus, the Son of God, came into the world;
and where sin abounded, grace superabounded;

---

[6] *Hom. in Annunt.*

whence death came, came life.
Life took the place of death.
He who through a woman became your Life, has routed death brought by woman.
As those whom Eve's flesh made only children of men,
those who are born anew of Mary's Son are called the children of God.

Hail, Mary! Full of grace!
Hail, reconciler of the world!
the seal of peace, the gate of life!
the entrance to paradise!

Blessed art thou among women.
You are the only one to escape the condemnation which all other women inherited:
"In sorrow shalt thou bring forth children," God said to Eve after her sin.[7]
You alone escape that other curse:
"Cursed be the barren woman in Israel."
On the contrary you receive a special blessing, not to live barren and yet to escape the sorrows of childbirth.
No other woman has received or ever will receive such a blessing.
For, when a woman becomes a mother, she forfeits her virginity;
if she remains a virgin, she cannot become a mother.
But you, Mary, you are at the same time both virgin and mother.
Some are mothers only; some are virgins only.
Your privilege is strictly your own; at the same time virgin and mother.
To you we may also apply Jesus' words:
"Mary has chosen the better part, which shall not be taken

---

7 Gen. 3:16.

away from her."[8]
Fruitfulness is a good thing;
virginity is the better part;
but the part most excellent is to be virgin and mother, the gift bestowed only upon the most holy Mother of God, the Virgin of virgins.[9]

Blessed art thou among women.
We shall always admire women blessed with fruitfulness, Sarah, Rachel and Rebecca, glorious springs of a noble people.
We shall always sing the praises of the virtuous woman, Naomi's daughter, Ruth the Moabite, for her virginal chastity.[10]
We shall always revere Judith, the widow, and her conquering might by which she cut off the head of Holofernes.
We shall always celebrate the incomparable wisdom of an Abigail, full of prudence,[11] and of Olda, daughter of Thecuath, who spoke to Yahweh.[12]
Who does not remember the matchless beauty of an Esther, who charmed Assuerus and overthrew the enemies of her people?[13]

In Holy Scripture types of Mary abound; they vie with one another in proclaiming her virtues, her greatness, her triumphs.
We have seen that she ineffably supplanted the ancient Eve;
    she excels beyond measure all the holy and courageous women whom the Holy Spirit has blessed.
She surpasses, we must admit, all those who will follow her down the ages to the end of the world.
And yet, among those are some great women, some greater than those of the Old Testament:
    saints, some beatified, others canonized;
    admirable virgins;
    courageous widows;

---

8 St. Luke 10:42.   9 St. Bernadine of Sienna: *De Salutatione Angelica.*
10 Ruth 2:11.   11 1 Kings 25:3.   12 2 Par. 34:22.
13 Esther 8, 9.

mothers, imitators of her loftiest virtues.
We name no one, so fearful are we of forgetting a single one.
But all those women together—what are they in comparison with you, Mary, Virgin and Mother?
Of all women you are the most beautiful, the most pure, the most generous, the most intrepid.

I have always admired so much that woman who bore your name—Mary, the sister of Moses and Aaron.
After you, she was, perhaps, the most renowned. She prefigured you as no other woman did.

>She was a virgin, a prophetess,
>who guided the people of Israel as they fled from Egypt, the accursed region of sin, through the Red Sea;
>the first woman ever to sing the immortal canticle: *Let us sing to the Lord!*

"Let us sing to the Lord: for He is gloriously magnified, the horse and the rider He hath thrown into the sea.
Pharaoh's chariots and his army He hath cast into the sea; his chosen captains are drowned in the Red Sea.
They are sunk to the bottom like a stone...
Who is like to Thee, among the strong, O Lord? who is like to Thee, glorious in holiness, terrible and praiseworthy, doing wonders?
In Thy mercy Thou hast been a leader to the people which Thou hast redeemed: and in Thy strength Thou hast carried them to Thy holy habitation."
So Mary the prophetess... took a timbrel in her hand: and all the women went forth after her with timbrels and with dances. And she began the song to them, saying: Let us sing to the Lord, for He is gloriously magnified, the horse and his rider He hath thrown into the sea.[14]

---

14 Cf. Exod. 15.

The figure leaps before our eyes:
It is you, Mary, Virgin and Mother. You precede the new people of God, freed from the chains of Satan and his horde, from his everlasting punishment.
You lead on the countless army of the elect through the Red Sea of the Blood of the Lamb, the blessed fruit of the glorious flock.
> You guide that army towards that promised land,
> where with Him we shall reign,
> where with you we shall triumph.

Yes, be ever blessed, powerful Cooperatrix, sole helper of the Redeemer!
Woman among all women, the only one worthy to lead us into heaven.
> Be ever blessed, loved and celebrated!
> With Jesus, the fruit of your virginal womb,
> you have conquered the world.

CHAPTER VI. BLESSED IS THE FRUIT OF THY WOMB, JESUS

1. THE VISITATION

GABRIEL, God's archangel, could but say to you, Mary: *Hail! blessed among women.*

You had not yet uttered your *fiat;* you had not yet, holy Virgin, accepted the honor of becoming God's Mother.
A woman, your cousin Elizabeth, until now barren, but by miracle made the mother of John whom she carries in her womb,
> merits the honor of chanting that canticle, so brief, yet so fraught with mystery:
> *Blessed is the fruit of thy womb.*

In that greeting is a world of marvels worthy of study.
Your *Visitation,* Mary, is another solemn commentary on the archangel's Salutation.
That Salutation coming from heaven must needs call forth another from earth.
But, no! the fact is that Elizabeth, in magnifying your greatness still more, struck the very same note of praise.
Mary had experienced within herself, so to speak, the power of the angel's *Ave.*
She "thought with herself"; her faith savored its content.
She remained humble, submissive, subject to the operation of the Holy Spirit, who made every word live for her.
The *Ave Maria* made an Immaculate Virgin the very Mother of

the Most High,
   of Him whose handmaid she wished to be and to remain.

At that moment the Word made flesh in Mary's virginal womb delivered the ineffable salutation:
   Hail, Mary! Full of grace, the Lord is with thee; blessed art thou among women.
He is with her; He is within her; henceforth He lives, He will speak and act through her.
He has become the divine Mover who enables her to perform under His impulse all the operations proper not only to God's Mother, but proper also and as a consequence to the Mother of men.

Mary, rising up![1] Look! she stands up, she rises for God's work.

Her cousin, Elizabeth, is by miracle six months with child. Gabriel so informs Mary.
The child in the womb of her who yesterday was barren, but whom God freed of her shame, is to be the first beneficiary of the *Ave* and of the wonders it has just effected.
John, son of Zachary and Elizabeth, needs Jesus Christ, but through Mary.
The ineffable mystery of the Incarnation of the Word in the womb of a virgin has as its object the destruction of the abominable monster, original sin.
Now, John, like all men past, present and future, is tainted with that sin.
John, of whom the same archangel has just predicted great things to Zachary,
   will be the first to be freed from Satan's bondage.
Why the first?
He is the greatest born of woman.
He is the immediate precursor of the Messias; it is only fitting

---
1 St. Luke 1:39.

that he receive the first outpouring of His grace.
Should he not be disposed beforehand by Him who from His Mother's womb comes to sanctify him?
John is the voice that is to announce the Word. The Word hurries to join the voice, to enrich it with the deep resonance which the breath of His grace will accord.

Mary goes in haste, to the hill country, to a city of Juda…
In her heart she holds the Eternal Word, filled with the fire and flame of His Father's bosom:
> the Word who brings Love's fire into this world.

He is hidden in His Mother's virginal womb, to transform her the very first in love divine.
But fire cannot stay shut in; it forces its way through everything; rather than remain trapped, it would melt rocks and overturn mountains.
So does the love which consumes Mary lift her over hills and mountains,
> to go and kindle in Elizabeth's house the fire that consumes her.

How that haste delights me! "With haste…."
You, Mary, have conceived the Word which the Father conceived in His bosom.
With that Word you wish to sanctify the voice of him who must in turn carry it, proclaim it, and avenge it.
With Him who is within you, you hasten towards that voice, because He will have you follow the trail of that giant;
> He impels you to advance with hurried steps.
> You hasten, and yet in what ecstasy you remain lost!
> In what union with your Child you make your way!

He who reigned eternally in His Father's bosom, as in the triumphal chariot which carries all His greatness, had His heart pierced by the sharpest of love's arrows.
With heart wounded by love He came down from the first char-

iot and passed immediately into a similar one.

Leaving His Father's bosom, He entered His admirable Mother's;

Through her He hastened to the aid of poor sinners.

Whither do You go, Lord, and what are You about to do?
As yet You are but an infant, and You hasten with hurried step to save us all from shipwreck.
As yet You cannot walk, but You use Your holy Mother's feet to come even unto me.

It is not so much she that carries You,

as that You carry her in her haste and lift her body over the hills.

You lift her soul even unto heaven.

Thus did Mary go...
She greeted Elizabeth.
What did she say to her? The Gospel does not tell us.
It is really not she who speaks.
The Word, made flesh in the womb of the Virgin of virgins, uses her tongue to speak to him who is His voice;

to him who lies near the heart of his holy mother, Elizabeth;

to John, who uses his mother's ears to hark to the adorable

Word speaking to him through Mary.

What did the Father's Word say to John?
A secret!
Doubtless He spoke to John tenderly; He penetrated the depths of his soul.
And Mary let go the shaft which struck John, on the instant transformed and sanctified, in the hitherto barren Elizabeth, and caused him to swoon for love.

For, "as soon as Elizabeth hears Mary's salutation,"

the infant in her womb pulsates with joy;

he stirs, he leaps;

he transmits to his mother, who encompasses him, the grace

and the joy with which he exults.
Both are inundated by the same torrent escaping from the Heart of God
> and hurling itself, through Mary the virginal conduit, on him and her whom heavenly consolations engulf.

Immediately Elizabeth, too, is filled with the Holy Spirit!
> Pause and consider those marvels:
> A Virgin-Mother, who carries God in her womb;
> a barren mother, who now carries in her womb him whom the Scripture more than once calls an angel.

By heeding an angel's *Ave,* Mary became the Mother of God;
Elizabeth, on hearing a Virgin speak, becomes an angel's mother.
> She who until now could bear only a sinner,
> becomes the mother of the greatest of saints.

Both Mary and Elizabeth, on receiving an angel's salutation, are filled with the Holy Spirit.
But in what different measure!

Elizabeth is filled with the Holy Spirit, that is, with His gifts and graces. Through the presence of the Saviour and His holy Mother she becomes holier,
> because she is nearer the spring and channel of grace.

Mary is filled, not only with the same grace, *full of grace,* but with the very Person of the Holy Spirit.
He becomes her particular possession, since He proceeds from the Word who is in the Virgin's womb.
She becomes His Spouse; He alone, her Spouse by His operation, renders her fruitful.
He is given to her, to dwell with her forever.
He and she are truly two in one flesh.

Elizabeth is the first to receive in a unique manner the power to understand something of the great mystery.
> "She cried out with a loud voice..."

Behold! like the prophets of old, all suddenly she sees!
like the Fathers and Doctors of the Church, she comprehends.
She is endowed with the intelligence of angels,
inflamed with the burning love of the seraphim.
Suddenly all the powers of her soul, all her body's energy,
her whole being, enriched by the gifts of the Holy Spirit,
becomes tense.

Animated by the divine breath, she bursts forth in tones so loud and strong, "with a loud voice," that even today after so many centuries that cry re-echoes in the Gospel.

That voice transmits to Mary our deep groanings, and to all those who love Mary her greeting to the Virgin Mother of God.

Blessed art thou among women, and blessed is the fruit of thy womb.

"And whence is this to me, that the mother of my Lord should come to me?

For behold as soon as the voice of thy salutation sounded in my ears, the infant in my womb leaped for joy.

And blessed art thou that hast believed, because those things shall be accomplished that were spoken to thee by the Lord.

And Mary said: *Magnificat!* My soul doth glorify, doth magnify the Lord!"[2]

2. ELIZABETH'S SALUTATION

Surely, *Mary,* your cousin Elizabeth was a prophetess, and, perhaps, the greatest prophetess of the New Testament.

As you entered her house with the gentleness of an angel and the majesty of a queen, she saw you and said to you:

Blessed art thou among women.

Who, pray, caused her to repeat literally the very same Saluta-

---

2 St. Luke 1: 43–46.

tion which Gabriel addressed to you?
Who prompted her to repeat that Ave which is your glory?

> She adds:
> *And blessed is the fruit of thy womb,*
> *And whence is this to me that the mother of my Lord should come to me?*

Who discloses to her of a sudden the heavenly secret, known only to you and Joseph, of what is happening to you?
Who told her that you are really the Mother of her God?
> and that the Infant close to your virginal heart is a Fruit, a Fruit of benediction,
> the Fruit of the new Eve, the Mother of the Living?
> the Fruit which must repair the disorder caused by the accursed and deathly fruit taken from the tree of the knowledge of good and evil?
> She said further:
> *Blessed art thou that hast believed,* believed so faithfully the angel's words.

You did not hesitate, like the Eve of perdition, to accept and obey the Lord's will;
> You answered: *Behold the handmaid of the Lord!*

Blessed indeed! You did not doubt or hesitate, as did Zachary, whose obstinacy God punished by striking him dumb.
No, *Mary!* You answered: *Fiat mihi! Be it done to me according to thy word.*
Who, then, revealed to Elizabeth that message of the angel and all its wonders, a message which no one on earth, not even the most holy, could have known?
Elizabeth was consecrated your prophetess, just as Zachary will soon appear as the herald of the Most High: *Blessed be the Lord God of Israel.*
Consecrated, I say, by the same Spirit of God that fills you both,
> who overflows from Jesus to you, and through you to John

himself.
Who can meditate enough on the words which that prophetess, so illustrious, so holy, introduces into the *Hail Mary*?
Words which redound to her glory and perpetuate her memory for nearly twenty centuries?
> words which will immortalize her forever?
> *Blessed is the fruit of thy womb!*

Behold, all that her faith recognizes in that ineffable mystery!
Ponder here those most important truths about the adorable Person of Jesus Christ, and
> the glory of His most holy Mother!

Elizabeth believes, and with a loud voice confesses the august dogmas of Mary's virginity and divine maternity.
With the same meaning that Gabriel gave to those words, she at first cries out:
> *Blessed art thou among women* that were, that are, that ever will be.

Why blessed?
Because she restores to life the first Eve, the guilty Eve.
Mary became the new Eve, created without stain, to become truly the Mother of the Living.
She is blessed because above all, quite otherwise than all other mothers who sacrifice the privilege of virginal integrity,
she alone preserved her privilege and can still and for all time be called the Virgin of virgins, all the while she is the Mother of the divine Child whom she bears.

> Ah, yes! that divine Child, true Son of God and true Son of Man,
> the Fruit of thy womb, blessed is He!
> Blessed, and why?
> Because He is the Blessed of all blessed;
> the same Blessed whom Zachary will now proclaim:
> "Blessed be the Lord God of Israel; because He hath visited

and wrought the redemption of His people."[3]
Elizabeth recognizes Him as such, so much so that in her humility she gives vent to her surprise:
> "And whence is this to me, that the mother of my God should come to me?"
> I feel so unworthy of such a visit!
> She who crosses the threshold of my house and in whose presence I now am
> is the Mother of my Lord, the Mother of my God!

I believe it... I admit it... I, His lowly creature, swoon in the presence of Him whom she bears.

> *Blessed is the fruit of thy womb.*
> O Mary, that God is really born of you,
> of your substance, of your virginal flesh.

In anticipation, all the infernal heresies, whether they strive in the course of the ages to belittle Christ's humanity by exalting His divinity,
> or to exalt His humanity by denying His divinity,
> at one fell stroke lie prostrate and confounded.

You are, *Mary,* truly the Mother of a Man who is and who remains always our God,
> God blessed forever and ever.

Elizabeth proclaims the two natures in Christ:
> the human nature, the only one which a virgin could give Him of her own substance;
> the divine nature, the only one which His Father communicated to Him from His own substance.

But those two natures are united in one and the same Person; not a human person, but a divine Person.
And, hence, *Mary* is truly the Mother of God.
Whatever may be said of the Son of the Father of heaven, may be said of the Virgin's Son:

---

3 St. Luke 1:68.

> He is the same and only Son of God.
> It is your glory, holy Elizabeth, that
> before the time and the decisions of general councils,
> before the Apostles,
> before the holy Fathers and Doctors of the Church,
> you declared that article of faith,
> and destroyed the monsters of heresy.

Who could have taught you that article of faith, if not the Holy Spirit within you?

> *Elizabeth was filled with the Holy Spirit.*

Surely you may well give way to cries, to raptures of joy, in which we join, when you say to Mary:
> *Blessed is the fruit of thy womb!*
> *Whence is this to me?* Adorable Providence! Whence this signal favor to me?
> Who obtains for me such a boon? The first visit which the Saviour of the world makes on earth,
> through the Virgin of virgins, the Mother of my God!

Dearest St. Elizabeth, you had prepared yourself for that visit. For six months you had remained hidden, stealing from the world and from all dealings with creatures. "She hid herself for six months."

> You did not waste time on the problems of your day;
> in the silence of your home in Hebron you lived a happy life!

But for the silence of that solitude, who knows? you might not have been honored with the visit of the Son of God,
> of that God borne in the innermost tabernacle of the Virgin Mother's womb.

How many graces you would have missed!

Through that visit, too, John himself, more solitary because secretly hidden in your miraculously fruitful womb, receives still more tremendous graces.

> O blessed solitude! Truly blessed solitude!

O Mary, if we would understand you aright, how much we should meditate on that crowning salutation!
And blessed is the fruit of thy womb, Jesus!

CHAPTER VII. JESUS

1. THE NAME ABOVE ALL NAMES

AND *blessed is the fruit of thy womb, Jesus.*
It remained for the Church, the heir of all God's inspirations, to declare that Name blessed forever.
She inserted it into the *Hail Mary,* inspired, as she always is, by the same Holy Spirit,
    who inspired the archangel Gabriel,
    and the prophetess, Elizabeth.

Ever after, the *Hail Mary* belongs to her; it belongs to every one of her children.
She is its guardian; she comments on it without ceasing; she disseminates it; she dispenses its rich and incomparable treasures.
She placed the holy name of Mary at the beginning of the Salutation as her divine commentary on all that that Salutation contains. It is the name of her who is full of grace, of her in whom the Lord dwells, whom God pervades with His power, wisdom and mercy. The name of His Mediatrix. It was to suggest and to lead up to the Name of Jesus.
It was to lead up to that Name as to the august climax of that Salutation, to be, as it were, its magnificent synthesis.

Mary,... and then, *Jesus.*
Always *Mary* first of all, then always and without cease, *Jesus.*

Hail, Mary! full of grace,

the Lord is with thee;
blessed art thou among women,
and blessed is the fruit of thy womb, Jesus, Christ our Lord.

Gabriel had announced to the humble, retiring Virgin:
"Thou shalt conceive ... and shalt bring forth a son; and thou shalt call his name, Jesus."

And, as the archangel uttered that Name before which every knee in heaven was already bowed,
that Name which soon all earth would adore,
which would make the denizens of hell quake with terror,
he etched it, he carved it, he engraved it, in flaming letters on Mary's Immaculate Heart.

As soon as she hears it uttered, she becomes calm and reassured. She remains silent; in rapture she listens as the angel proclaims the greatness of that Name, "holy and terrible," as the Church calls it.[1] She falls into an ecstasy, swept away by the intense illumination, by the burning flames of that Name of the Man-God. She allows herself to melt therein with love.

She is consumed by that fire coming down from heaven into her virginal womb.

In that act of contemplation, the first act of praise and adoration of the most sacred Name of the Son of God,
she conceives the Son of Man, her Son, with the words:
"*Ecce!* Behold! *Fiat mihi!* Be it done!"
That Name! She keeps it secret.

She does not reveal it even to Joseph, the Just One, her chaste spouse.

He will learn it after some months, when the angel, the same angel, doubtless, appears to him,
to reassure him and persuade him to take without hesitating the hand of the Virgin of virgins,
the hand of her who is now the Mother of his God.

---

1 Ant., Feast of the Holy Name of Jesus.

As soon as he hears His Name who is conceived of the Holy Spirit in the virginal womb,
> he is reassured; he calmly submits.
> He takes Mary as his spouse, he and she both virgins.
> Mary remains silent;
> Joseph also holds his peace.

That sacrosanct Name of Jesus, hidden from eternity in the bosom of the Blessed Trinity,
> that Name, proposed from the beginning to the angelic hierarchies for acknowledgment and adoration,
> the Name of their God, the Name which is the source of their graces and of their own salvation,
> we might say that Mary and Joseph did not dare—so heavenly and so dread did they feel that Name to be—
> although it was laden with the infinite mercy of a Saviour we might say that as yet they dared not bring it to their lips, or yet disclose it to sinful man, so little prepared to hear it and to receive its ineffable influence.

Nevertheless, scarcely was He born who bears that Name, *Jesus,*
> scarcely had He uttered a cry on the cold manger straw of the midnight cave,
> when the angel of the Lord—always Gabriel, the Angel of the Incarnation, we feel sure—shattered the night air with the revelation of that Name, *Jesus,*
> to the lowly shepherds, surrounded by his brilliant light:
> "Behold, I bring you good tidings of great joy that shall be to all the people:
> For, this day is born to you a Saviour, who is Christ the Lord."[2]
> Yes, a Saviour, *Jesus!*
> He will do what His Name signifies.
> He will deliver His people, and all the people from sin.
> He will save all men.
> "Fear not." He who bears that Name "is an infant, wrapped

---

[2] St. Luke 2: 10–11.

in swaddling-clothes and laid in a manger."
If His Name is "holy and terrible,"[3]
it is also overflowing with sweetness, goodness and mercy.
It is a Name which brings grace,
a Name which opens the door to eternal life.

That is why in that night's darkness in which the peoples, which that Name was to save, were still engulfed,
the multitude of angels with Gabriel sang:
"Glory to God in the highest,
and on earth peace to men of good will."[4]

The sacrosanct Name of the Saviour, *Jesus,* is just that and all that:
Glory given to God on high,
in the peace which it brings to men.

2. THE POWER OF THAT NAME

And blessed is the fruit of thy womb, Jesus.
We can never tire of repeating those words.
Finger the beads of your rosary! On each bead repeat fifty, one hundred and fifty times, only this:

Hail, Mary! full of grace.
And as often say and savor:
And blessed is the fruit of thy womb, Jesus.

Bit by bit those words enter into the soul; they penetrate its very depths;
they slip into its marrow, if we may so speak, like an oil poured out;[5]
a sweet and soothing oil poured out plentifully and over all, an oil which brightens, nourishes, sweetens the soul.

---

3 Ps.110:9.   4 St. Luke 2:14.   5 Cant. 1:2.

Say even less than that; say simply
Jesus!
That word brightens, and like food nourishes, like a medicine sweetens, everything.
Jesus! That Name holds so much lustre that it infallibly communicates light, especially the light of faith.
   Suddenly the darkened intellect returns to the light of its day,[6]
Jesus, God of God, Light of Light, to become Light in the Lord.[7]
Jesus! what support, what strength in that very thought!
   It reanimates the prostrate senses,
   strengthens virtue, invigorates morality,
   sustains chaste affections!
How dry and tasteless the soul's food, if not sprinkled, penetrated with that soothing oil!
How vapid, lacking that heavenly seasoning!
Place, inscribe the Name of Jesus in your writings, if you want me to relish them.
   Jesus! That honey in the mouth, that melody in the ear, that thrill of joy in a soul!
   Jesus! Jesus! Jesus!
Make that Name your medicine, a universal remedy. There is no better.
You are sad, my soul; afflicted, unable to do more!
Utter that Name: *Jesus*...every cloud disappears.
You feel weighted down by sin, frightened, perhaps;
despair pursues you...what will you do?
Ah! repeat again and again: *Jesus! Jesus!*
That Name, of all names most sacred,
   heals envy's wound,
   stays impurity's every motion,
   extinguishes the fires of base passion,

---

6 1 Thess. 5:5.   7 Ephes. 5:8.

quenches the thirst of greed,
subdues the surge of all my evil instincts.

I cannot think of or utter *Jesus,* without bringing my mind straightway to dwell on Him,
on a Man meek and humble of heart,
exceedingly good, moderate, chaste, merciful beyond measure; in a word, on One I know and adore in all purity, all holiness.
I name Him who is at once God and Man.

O my soul, repeat to yourself unceasingly: *Jesus.*
May your Name, dear Saviour, be and remain always, with that of Mary, my only riches!
Put both your names as a seal on my heart,
as a seal on my arm.[8]
Let me absorb from them the love with which I wish to love You and the strength which must uphold me.
All those thoughts and feelings... I do not invent them. They are the thoughts and feeling of all God's saints; of St. Bernard, in particular, who
has studied, honored and celebrated, as no one else has, the sacrosanct Name of *Jesus,*
and the holy name of *Mary.*

Jesus!
We may ask ourselves why in view of the names which the well-known prophecies give the Virgin's future Child—Emmanuel, Admirable, Counsellor, Mighty God, Father of the world to come, Prince of Peace,[9] the Lord our Just One[10]... why we prefer to call Him *Jesus.*

All those other names were but figures; their reality is expressed clearly in the one Name, *Jesus.*
They were, if you wish, random strokes of the brush, which,

---

8 Cant. 8:6.   9 Is. 7:14.   10 Jer. 33:16.

taken together, were meant to express the adorable Name which He bears. That Name includes all those various names.
It surpasses them in sweetness, excellence, strength, majesty.
It is, as it were, the soul, the quintessence of all that the prophets tried to say of Him in all those different titles which they assigned to Him.
Jesus! that Name expresses more than *Emmanuel,* God with us.
Jesus means God with us, and we with God,
> for it signifies the ineffable union of the two natures, the divine and the human, in one and the same Person.

It signifies more than Admirable; it signifies adorable;
> more than Counsellor; it signifies the Infinite Wisdom of God the Father;
>
> more than God; it signifies at one and the same time Man and God;
>
> more than Mighty, since it signifies God's almighty strength;
>
> more than Father of the world to come, for it connotes neither past nor future; it signifies God eternal;
>
> more than Prince of Peace, since it signifies peace itself and our reconciliation with God His Father;
>
> more than the Lord our Just One, since He is our Justice, our sanctification itself.[11]

I shall never sufficiently grasp what the Name of *Jesus* contains, what it brings me, promises me,
and all that it guarantees for time and eternity.

> *And blessed is the fruit of thy womb, Jesus.*

O Mary, I end your Salutation with that Name.
You alone, who uttered it for the first time in your inmost soul on the sacred day of your Annunciation, can carve and engrave on my heart in flaming letters: *Jesus.*
I understand why many saints, like Jeanne de Chantal, had it imprinted on their breast, branded on their living flesh.

---

11 1 Cor. 1:30.

The saints know how to be heroic when the Holy Spirit moves them and inflames them to a love that torments them.

O Mary, Mother of God, Virgin of virgins, you first etched that Name deep in their souls. That was the essential thing.
Indeed, it suffices for most of those to whom you have given *Jesus.* That is the grace which, fittingly, I beg of your motherly goodness, each time I recite my *Ave.*
Ah, yes! that is enough for me, and I appreciate it more than I can say.

As the Sacred Liturgy sings so admirably with St. Bernard, the Name of Jesus is always a sweet memory.[12]
So may it be to me, even as the presence of Jesus Himself, which charms, expands and pacifies me.

Jesus!
>no song can be sweeter,
>no word more pleasing to my ear,
>no thought more expansive to my heart,
>than *Jesus,* Son of God.

Jesus!
>hope of those who repent,
>mercy for those who ask it,
>goodness showing itself to those who seek You...
>and who will say what You are to those who find You?

Try, my lips, to tell what it is to love the Name of *Jesus.*
Only he who experiences that love can describe it!
The moment I utter Your Name, Your truth flashes before my soul's eyes.
For Your sake I begin to despise all worldly vanity,
and to burn with the flame of Your eternal love.

O Jesus! song so sweet to my ears,

---

12 St. Bernard: *Jesu Dulcis Memoria.*

honey so delicious to my mouth,
heavenly nectar for my heart!
tasting You, I hunger still;
imbibing You, I still thirst;
ever I long for You more, longing for nothing else.

O most sweet *Jesus,* hope of my soul, which sighs for You, behold my tears, they entreat You!
listen to my inmost cries, they call to You!
stay with me, with all of us, Lord,
"because it is towards evening and the day is now far spent."

Jesus, matchless Flower of a Virgin-Mother,
Love, full of sweetness, enduring fire of most ardent longings,
all praise and honor to Your Name on earth and in the kingdom of Your blessedness!

O Mary, how worthily it was said of you that day:
And blessed is the fruit of thy womb, Jesus![13]
I can add nothing to your praise.
I can do no more than cast myself at your feet and henceforth confident beyond measure, with hands folded in prayer, repeat to you:

> *Holy Mary, Mother of God,*
> *pray for us sinners,*
> *now and at the hour of*
> *our death.*
> *Amen*

---

[13] Cf. Dom Vandeur, *"Jesus"*—*Elévations sur son amitié.*

PART TWO: THE INVOCATION

HOLY MARY, MOTHER OF GOD,
PRAY FOR US SINNERS,
NOW AND AT THE HOUR
OF OUR DEATH.
AMEN.

CHAPTER VIII. HOLY MARY

1. HER HOLINESS

Holy *Mary! Mother of God.*
After meditating on the archangel's *Ave,* the Church stands enraptured before the greatness of her whom Gabriel saluted,
and in one great cry of her heart sums up all the Virgin's praises in:
Holy Mary! Mother of God.
In these words we recognize the whole content of Marian theology.

Holy Mary!
Virgin Mother, holiest of all the holy ones of God, holiest treasure-house of all holiness![1]
The prophet tells us that God is "wonderful in His saints."[2]
How wonderful, then, He must be in the Mother of the Saint of saints!
In her to an eminent degree all the privileges of other saints meet. The Greek Church calls her *Panagia,* the all holy. It is, as it were, the proper name of Mary, Mother of God, her name par excellence. To the Christians of the Western Church her most common title is Holy Virgin.
It is again the proper name of Mary, a title reserved to the Mother of God.
The Church venerates many holy virgins, martyrs and other

---

1 St. Andrew of Crete: *Hom. I de Virg. domit.*   2 Ps. 67:36.

saints, whose heroic virtues perfume the vineyard of the Father, but no one of them has merited or obtained the title, Holy Virgin.

Whatever of sanctity, of dignity, of merit, of grace, and of glory, that we can imagine, all is in Mary, the Holy Virgin.

Holiness is a complete separation from creatures and perfect union with the Creator.

A saint is a soul which retires into God, absorbed only in Him, in His wisdom, His love, His beauty, His beatitude.

In that absorption he or she resembles God, the Holy of Holies, the One pre-eminently separated from all that is not Himself.

Prostrate in adoration before Him, the seraphim sing:

> Holy, holy, holy is the Lord, God of hosts![3]

Their song expresses the inaccessibility of that God hidden in His infinite essence,

> in His infinite purity, His infinite detachment from every created being,
>
> His infinite absorption in Himself.

Every last wonder of God's countless wonders is contained in that epithet of praise: the Holy.

And that Holy is Mary's Son.

Moreover, only *Mary*, the Mother of God, can, after her divine Son, be called thrice holy.

The Church likes to dwell on that thought.

In her *Ave* she calls her Holy Mary; and in the well-known Litanies she always begins:

> Holy Mary...
>
> Holy Mother of God, Holy Virgin of virgins...

Her wish has been to penetrate and saturate the mind and heart with reminders of such unique holiness.

From the first moment of her Immaculate Conception in the womb of her mother, St. Anne, *Mary* was singularly set apart,

---

[3] Is. 6:13.

withdrawn, hidden in God, far from every creature.
She was and she still is the true solitary, finding in her God a vast solitude.
Her holiness is the wall which keeps her removed from all other creatures.
Mary's heart was hidden and remains hidden in Jesus Christ, and the Heart of Jesus Christ abides in *Mary*.
Those Hearts are each other's treasure-house.
The Saint of saints belongs entirely to the holiest among women; the holiest among women belongs entirely to the Saint of saints.
Who has ever seen or heard the like?
Think of it! God enclosed in a Virgin's womb;
> in a womb so pure, so immaculate that it becomes the Holy of Holies, in which Jesus Christ our Lord, the High Priest, alone found entrance.

That womb became the Temple of the divine Priest, the golden altar, the propitiatory of the New Testament, the Ark of our very sanctification.
Is it any wonder that that heavenly creature was of necessity an ocean of holiness?
In her, in her every condition and every mystery we see only God. Her holiness is the mark which distinguishes her from all other creatures.
She is entirely for God, for Him alone.
Doubtless, she loves to be called the Mother and the Virgin of the poor, the Mediatrix and Dispenser of grace and of all mercy;
> but only in view of an unceasing intimate union with God, and without prejudice to that sublime union and her separation from every creature. That is sufficient for her.

Of her Holy Scripture could declare that "all the rivers run into the sea, and the sea doth not overflow";[4]
> just so, all the virtues of the saints meet in Mary without overflowing, without even equalling the ocean of her holiness.

---

4 Eccl. 1:7.

God raised her so high in Himself that He never created, never will create a greater,
> a holier person more worthy of Himself, of His greatness, His love, than that divine Mother.

In the order of grace and holiness among creatures, she is the term of all the operations, all the effects, all the communications and outpourings of His power, wisdom and goodness.

Having carried within her Jesus Christ, the Holy of God,
> she shares, as no one else, in her divine Son's holiness.

She comes nearest to the holiness of God.

St. Anselm, that renowned servant of Mary and Doctor of the Church, has written:

> "It was fitting that she, in whose bosom the conception of a Man-God was to take place, should be a mother most pure; it was fitting that from then on she should be resplendent with the most complete holiness that can be conceived after that of God.
>
> God the Father decided to give her His only Son, the Son who was equal to Him and begotten of His Heart, whom He loved as Himself,
>
> to give her Him in such a way that He was the one and only Son common to the Father and that Virgin.
>
> The Son chose her as His Mother according to the flesh;
>
> and the Holy Spirit fittingly willed to operate in her, that she might conceive and bear the Word from whom He Himself proceeds."[5]

What more? We dare only repeat:
> *Holy Mary!*

There is such charm, such sweetness, such grace in repeating it! Christian soul, continue to finger the beads of your rosary, and say only that:
> *Holy Mary!*

---

5 *De Concep. Virg.* 17.

While you are doing it, think! she is the holiest of women, the Virgin-Mother thrice holy,
> because she is holy of the Father, holy of the Son, holy of the Holy Spirit of Love.
>
> You will relish more the sweetness of her *Ave;*
> you will feel, as it were, carried away by her holiness;
> you will long more and more to become holy and to say to her:
> *Holy Mary, Mother of God, holy Virgin of virgins!*

2. HER VIRTUES

How wisely the Church acted in joining those two words together!
> *Holy Mary!*

Truly, the Church wishes to remind us, each time we say the Hail Mary, that holiness and Mary are synonymous.

Hail Mary. Thus we begin the Angelic Salutation; all that follows is a development in wondrous wise, as we have seen, of what *Mary* is,
> of what that sweet name recalls to us—the number and magnitude of her gifts, all that she possesses of the grace and presence of God, of blessings of every kind.

We then understand that she is truly holy, the holiest among women,
> the holiest after Him who is the Holy of Holies.

Holy Mary.
I could wish to enumerate here all her gifts, all her virtues;
I could wish I were able to show how the Holy Spirit overshadowed her
> with filial fear of the Lord, incomparable piety, heroic fortitude, most prudent counsel, fulness of knowledge, profound understanding, and divine wisdom.

I could wish with St. Bernardine of Siena to meditate on her twelve principal virtues,
> which he calls her "maids of honor," who abide with her always and accompany her everywhere:
>
> her reserve, her silence, her modesty, her prudence, her fear of the Lord, her purity, her diligence, her charity, her obedience, her humility, her right intention, her faith.[6]

Those virtues adorned her when the archangel Gabriel came down to visit her; they rendered her forever beautiful.

But I cannot. I feel unequal to the task. These pages do not pretend to furnish theologians and doctors with a new Mariology. My aim is much more modest; I am trying to reach many small souls, for whom a few rays of Holy Mary's beauty will suffice;
> that they may endlessly admire and better pronounce her name—after the Name of Jesus, the most beautiful of names.

I shall recall only that passage of Holy Scripture in which the Holy Spirit tells us:
> "Wisdom hath built herself a house, she hath hewn her out seven pillars."[7]

The text speaks of wisdom from heaven, the wisdom of Christ; the Power of God, and His Wisdom,[8] who chose Mary's womb as His house;
> the house of a most pure, most chaste, most inviolable Virgin;
> the house of her of whom the Holy Spirit says:

"When I go into my house, I shall repose myself with her."[9]

Wisdom has reposed in that house of seven pillars.

The seven pillars are:

the four cardinal virtues—prudence, temperance, fortitude, justice;

and the three theological virtues—faith, hope and charity.

That house of God, the gate of heaven, is adorned with the admi-

---

6 *De. laud. Virginitatis,* Serrn. 48. 7 Prov. 9:1.
8 1 Cor. 1:30. 9 Wis. 8:16.

rable train of all the moral virtues,
> with the twelve fruits of the Holy Spirit and the eight beatitudes, as they are found in no other saint.
> What a palace! what splendor! what gold and diamonds!
> *Mary* was created the abode of virtue,
> the unfailing source of divine illuminations.

Moreover, the holy Fathers and most learned Doctors were unable to give expression to the length, the breadth, the depth, the height—
> indefinite measurements they are of the perfection and holiness of *Holy Mary*.

They called her
> a special world belonging to God;
> a heaven, God's heaven, the heaven of heavens belonging to the Lord;
> the loftiest, the richest dwelling possessed by God;
> the house of incorruptible wood;
> the house of gold, the palace spacious, containing Him whom the universe cannot contain;
> the immeasurable abode wherein the Infinite resides;
> the august and sacred sanctuary in which dwells the fulness of divinity;
> the supreme Ark of divine majesty;
> the only temple worthy of the Almighty.[10]

We forego enumerating the titles which accrue to *Holy Mary* and her virtues.
> It remains for me only to cry out to her:
> *Thou art all fair, Mary, and there is not a spot in thee,*[11]
> no sin, no stain, no imperfection.
> You are, *Holy One*, a "pure emanation of the glory of Almighty God,"[12]
> of that beloved Son, born of your virginal womb, who makes

---

10 de Lornbaerde: *Pourquoi j'aime Marie*, p. 138.   11 Cant. 4:7.
12 Wis. 7:25.

you
Holy Mary, Mother of God.
Just as to know the eternal Father, I cast my gaze on that Son, so, to know Jesus, I cast my gaze on you, *Holy One.*
Draw us with the perfume of your virtues;
"the smell of thy garments is as the smell of frankincense."[13]
May that perfume waft us on high, to heaven, to God!

---

13 Cant. 4:11.

CHAPTER IX. MOTHER OF GOD

1. HER VIRGINITY

Holy *Mary, Mother of God, Holy Virgin of Virgins.* Many centuries before Gabriel, Mary's archangel, appeared to deliver his *Ave,* Isaias had prophesied:
"Behold, a virgin shall conceive."[1]

Draw near, ye patriarchs and prophets, Israel and all the nations of the world:
look, listen, and be amazed!
Behold that new wonder, the most stupendous marvel of the ages!
the masterpiece of God's omnipotent hand!
a virgin shall conceive and bear a Son!
That Virgin is God's Daughter, Mother, Spouse.
She will be Queen of angels and Mother of men.
She will unite God to man, heaven to earth, motherhood to virginity.
She will lead sinners to sanctity!

"It was fitting that the holy flesh of the Saviour should, as it were, be adorned with all the purity of virginal blood,
that it might be worthy of union with the Word of God."[2]
Tertullian had said: "It was fitting that the Son of God should be born of woman, so as to be Son of Man;

---

[1] Is. 7:14.   [2] Bossuet: *2eme Serm. sur la Conc. de la Vierge.*

that He be born not through man's operation, lest, as Son of Man, He seem not to be Son of God."³

Behold, the wise provision! how wonderful it was!

Mary's motherhood accounts for the humanity of the Word; her virginity is earnest of His divinity.

Mother-Virgin corresponds with Man-God.
Mary is a virgin, yet a mother;
she is a mother, yet remains a virgin.⁴
The crowning glory of virginity is in such a motherhood.

Your conception and bearing of a Son, *Mary*, far from destroying your virginity, sets the seal upon it.

You are more a virgin than a mother,
since you are the mother of virginity's author.
You are more a mother than a virgin,
since you are both to the highest degree and in a double sense.
You are twice a mother, being Mother-Virgin;
you are twice a virgin, being Virgin-Mother.
Things which otherwise exclude each other, meet and multiply in you.
Thus you offer to the world, more particularly to your own sex, the most marvelous, most adorable masterpiece of virginity and motherhood.

A Virgin-Mother!

That is my faith! I believe that Jesus Christ was conceived by the power of the Holy Spirit and born of the Virgin Mary.⁵

O Mary, Virgin in conceiving, Virgin in bearing your Son, and after His birth still a Virgin! I believe it!

How I love that passage of St. Augustine:

"Jesus Christ, begotten of the Father from eternity, was born of the Virgin Mother.

In His first nativity He was begotten of the Father, who re-

---

3 *De Carne Christi.*
4 Aug. Nicholas: *Economie de l'Incarn.*, II, 4.   5 Apostles' Creed.

mained without change;
in the second He was born of a Virgin who remained without stain.
The Father, who begot Him, was alone responsible for the first nativity;
the Virgin Mother without stain, who knew not man, was alone the author of the second.
In the Father, perpetual divinity;
in the Mother, eternal virginity.
'I will espouse thee to me forever,'[6] God said to Mary through His prophet.
Now, she who is the eternal spouse of a God must be eternally a virgin.
Jesus Christ comes invisibly from the Father, from the Mother in visible form.
From the Father He comes in a mysterious way;
He is born of the Mother in an incomparable way;
because in His first nativity He has, without corruption, God for Father ... and no mother;
in His second, He has a Virgin for mother ... and no father.
From His Mother's womb, which He created, He issues without corrupting it, in order that He, who has in heaven as Father a Virgin-God, may have on earth a Virgin as Mother."[7]

How well I understand the endless praise which the great saints and doctors of the Church bestowed on her, who, virgin in body, virgin in soul, virgin in heart, is the Queen of virgins!

St. Gregory calls her the standard-bearer of virginity;
St. Ambrose, the mistress of virginity;
St. John Damascene, the glory of virginity;
St. Germain, the type and model of virginity;
St. James in his liturgy, the glory of virgins.
St. Bernard declares that Mary's virginity surpasses the pu-

---

6 Osee 2: 19.   7 *Serm. 18 in Natali Domini.*

rity of angels.[8]
St. Epiphanius teaches that the use of the title Holy Virgin, as her proper and distinctive name, is essential to Mary,
   that it is a constant and perduring custom in the Church.
The Eastern Christians call her, as the ancient Latin Fathers did, by a single word, *Ever-Virgin, Sempervirgo.*

What more can we do, but sing with the Church, as if Mary were virginity incarnate:
   "O Holy Virginity! what praise I can offer thee, I know not; for, Him whom the heavens cannot contain, thou hast borne. in thy bosom."[9]
We should really here inscribe in letters of gold the Godlike testimony which the lips of that woman of the Gospel rendered to Mary, Virgin and Mother.
Raising her voice from the crowd, she cried out to Jesus:
   "Blessed is the womb that bore thee and the paps that gave thee suck."[10]

In that cry the ages jealously profess and celebrate their faith in Mary's divine motherhood.
Jesus did not scorn that testimony to His Mother.
On the contrary, He enhanced it still more, when, in answer to that woman, He said:
   "Yea, rather, blessed are they who hear the word of God and keep it."[11]
That Word of God is the Incarnate Word, the Word made flesh in *Mary.*
It made her first of all mother according to the spirit, before she became mother according to the flesh.
For, you conceived that Word, *Mary,* according to the spirit in your soul, before you conceived Him in your womb.
You conceived Him first by faith: "Blessed art thou that hast

---

8 *De Concept. Virg.,* ch. 18.
10 St. Luke 11:27.
9 Resp. of Matins, Off. B.M.V.
11 *Ibid.,* 28.

believed," Elizabeth said.
> You are mother, because faith made you fruitful.
> Thus all the holy doctors teach.[12]

Your motherhood according to the flesh is an unparalleled elevation, a source of great glory;
> and yet, the holy doctors insist, more glorious still is your spiritual motherhood.

The eminent Suarez goes so far as to say with St. Justin that you are more blessed because of the virtues which render you worthy of the divine maternity, than because of the dignity itself of being the Mother of God.[13]

That motherhood was, to be sure, a gratuitous gift, but, if you are the Mother of God, it is also because of your virtues.
> We can understand the Apostle's words:
> "That Christ may dwell by faith in your hearts."[14]

Jesus' answer to the woman in the Gospel, *Mary*, enhanced your praise.

What consolation you afford to those millions and millions of souls, who, by imitating you, preserve and consecrate to God their holy virginity!
> Ye holy virgins of every time and place,
> ye virgins of every age,
> ye virgin martyrs, and ye virgins who live out a long and glorious martyrdom,
> rejoice! a Virgin gave birth to Christ.

May barrenness not afflict you! Your faith affords a more blessed and more glorious fruitfulness.

While living the life of virgins, you conceive, you generate Christ spiritually,
> and in that Christ a countless number of souls,
> without sacrificing your integrity.

Imitate faithfully the Mother of your heavenly Spouse!

---

12 St. Aug. *Lib. de S. Virgine,* ch. III.
13 *In III S. Th. q. 7, disp. I, s. 2.*   14 Eph. 3:17.

He who was born of her does not deny you the signal honor of a fruitful virginity.

> That which He gave to a mother, to a holy virgin,
> that which He retains in His own most pure flesh,
> He will give to you, that you may be virgins and mothers;
> that your flesh may be likened to His holy flesh,
> free from stain.

Come to *Mary,* and you will always be virgins; you will always be fruitful.

Happy, all ye, who unceasingly heed the whisperings of the Word whom the Father conceives and begets in eternity!

Happy ye, who receive that Word in your inmost hearts, who conceive and engender Him in yourselves,

> in order to conceive and engender Him anew in others!
> "O Holy Virginity, truly I know not what praise to offer thee!"[15]
> Mary and thou, you two are identical.

The great Apostle has said: "A virgin thinketh on the things of the Lord, that she may be holy both in body and spirit."[16]

O Virginity, thou art so sublime a virtue that the name "virgin" springs from virtue as its root.[17]

To seek what thou choosest to imitate on earth, thou hast gone to heaven. And, raising thyself above the clouds and the firmament, thou hast penetrated even unto God;

> thou hast found in that same Father's bosom the Incarnate Word.[18]
> To be a virgin and an angel is one and the same thing....[19]

The virgin differs from the angel in bliss, in happiness, but not in virtue.

The angel's virginity is more blissful; the virgin's more heroic. To be a virgin is a reward won through courage, a courage which

---

15 Resp. of Off.   16 1 Cor. 7:34.
17 St. Fulgentius: *Epist.* 3, ch. 4.
18 St. Ambrose: *De Institutione Virg.*, ch. 15.
19 St. Gregory: *De Virginitate.*

acquires by grace what the angel possesses by nature.
O Virginity, thou art so great, so wondrous a thing that thou makest the soul like to the incorruptible God.[20]

A virgin is the living vessel of Jesus Christ.[21]

"And yet," exclaims St. Bernard, "do not glorify thyself because of thy bodily chastity, though it be so praiseworthy a virtue.

"The higher thou art raised, the more shouldst thou humble thyself in everything,

if thou wishest, like *Mary,* to find grace with God."

That which the Lord regarded in her was not her chastity; it was the humility of His handmaid.

God alone bestows and safeguards virginity, and that among the humble.

Hail, Mary, full of grace.
Holy Mother of God,
Holy Virgin of virgins,
you are the Vessel of Honor, in which the Father of heaven wished you to safeguard His Word;
the Spiritual Vessel, the Vessel of the Holy Spirit, who caused you to blossom with all the virtues that might warrant your encompassing Him;
the Vessel of Singular Devotion, consecrated wholly to the Incarnate Word, the Redeemer,
to cooperate with Him in the signal task of our redemption, our salvation.
O beautiful Virgin! most beautiful, most pure, most chaste, most immaculate Virgin,
may angels proclaim you, saints sing your praise, virgins imitate you!
You are virginity's crown and glory!

---

20 St. Basil: *De Vera Virginitate.*   21 St. Basil *De laud. Virg.*

2. THE GREAT MYSTERY

Holy Mary, Mother of God.
The Motherhood of *Mary!* The foundation of all her greatness, of all her prerogatives;
of her predestination from eternity, her Immaculate Conception, her titles of Co-Redemptrix, Dispenser of grace,
her joys, her sorrows, her glory!
"Mary is God's Mother!" said Bossuet. "That embraces all. It says everything."

To be God's Mother! Such a sublime participation in the Divinity, a union so strong that above Mary we find only God!
St. Thomas has well said: "Between God the Father and the Mother of the Word exists a special affinity.
"The Paternity of God the Father and the Motherhood of the Virgin-Mother resemble each other so strongly, and approach each other so nearly, they are so closely bound one with the other, that one touches the other."[22]

Mother of God.
That title contains inexhaustible treasure.
To be God's Mother! To have given Him along with His human nature, her own substance, her body, her flesh, her blood;
to acquire over Him rights which a mother exercises over her child, over her descendants;
to find Him subject to her as a son, so much so that He calls her mother, respects her, honors her, loves and obeys her as His mother.
Such are the stupendous relations existing between Jesus and Mary. While He lives nine months in her womb, the same blood circulates in Him and her,
the same blood for her and Jesus;
their hearts beat with the same pulsations,

---

22 *S. Th.*, II-II, q. 103, a 4.

the same breath quickens the flame.
More than that, Mary's blood, the substance out of which was formed the precious body of Jesus, and the milk with which she nourished Him, which also became part of the substance of the Son, were, so to speak, hypostatically united with the eternal Word.
St. Augustine concludes: "Jesus' flesh is Mary's flesh. In giving us His body as food and His precious blood as drink, He gives us the body, the blood, the milk and the substance of the Virgin Mary, converted into His very own substance."[23]

> *Mother of God!* Yes, because He, who is your son in time, is also in eternity the Father's Son;
> I mean that both are united in the same Person.
> The mother of the Person of the Word is really the *Mother of God.*

No dignity approaches nearer to the hypostatic union of the two natures in Jesus than does that of the divine motherhood. That is why great theologians teach that the divine motherhood belongs to the order of the hypostatic union and possesses an essential relation to it;

> so much so that *Mary, the Mother of God,* could be no more intimately united with God without seeming to be herself God.
> With reason, then, can Mary exclaim in her *Magnificat:*
> "He who is mighty hath done great things to me."
> Great things for me, yes, and also for Him who did them.

Those things are so great that *Mary* herself, doubtless, could not fully understand their greatness.
The Blessed Trinity alone can comprehend the height of that dignity.
And St. Bernard can declare: "To be *Mother of God* is so great a grace that God could not offer a greater."
"True, He can make the earth and the heavens greater, but

---

23 *De Assump. Virg.*

He cannot add to the dignity of His Mother."[24]

O wonder of wonders! Mary, *Mother of God!*

That God should beget God is conformable to the divine nature; it is necessary in order that God be God.

But that a woman should conceive and bear a God, that is the marvel of marvels!

That is what we believe and say and celebrate, when on our knees we repeat with the ages, and will repeat into eternity:

> "I believe in *One Lord Jesus Christ,*
> the only Son of God, begotten of the Father from eternity...
> God of God, Light of Light, true God of true God...
> Who took flesh by the operation of the Holy Spirit,
> *in the womb of the Virgin Mary;*
> and He became Man."[25]

3. MOTHER OF MEN

The title, Mother of God, logically and theologically connotes the title, *Mother of Men.*

> *O Mary,* you are *Mother of God,* and for that reason *Our Mother.*
> For us, what grace and good fortune!
> *Mary* is the Mother of my God, and for that reason, in the true sense of the word, I salute my own Mother... *Ave! Hail!*

Holy Spirit of the Father and the Son, who overshadowed Mary to make her Mother of God and my Mother, teach me well that consoling, that wondrous lesson!

> *Mary, Mother of God and Mother of Men.*
> Who are You, Lord Jesus?
> Essentially the Saviour, the Redeemer;
> You are our Mediator with the Father.
> In a word, You are, as the Apostle teaches:

---

24 *Spec. B.M.V.,* lect. 10.   25 Credo of the Mass.

"The head of the body of the church,"[26]

"the Son, ... first-born amongst many brethren."[27]

All Christians are your members; in the multitude which they compose, in which they are one, You are their elder brother. Essentially You are that; You are, of necessity, the first.

If the Incarnation of your Person, O Word of God, must redeem and save men, You are necessarily their Mediator, their First-born, the august Head of the Mystical Body, Your Church.

Mystical does not mean unreal; it means only that the Church is not the physical body of Christ.

Numerous are the things which are not seen, but which still are real, whose existence no one in his senses doubts, for instance, the existence of God and His angels.

> Jesus, You are our Priest, the High Priest of the whole human race,
>
> the Mediating Lamb, immolated "before the foundation of the world."[28]

It is that Jesus, not an abstract, but a very concrete Christ, whom we adore.

He is united, necessarily, to each one of us, as the head is united to each and every member of the body, to transmit the life-stream which conserves, nourishes and directs it.

> Of that Head, Mary, Mother of God, is the true Mother.

Mary, Mother of Jesus, you are our Mother!

You bring forth the Head. In Him you engender us also; mystically, it is true, but really—all the members whom He wishes to vivify.

> In Jesus, whose Mother you are, we are included;
>
> all men, past, present and yet to be, all who aspire to redemption are contained in Him, at least virtually.

To exclude us would be to belittle your motherhood.

> In conceiving Jesus, in giving Him birth, you conceived and

---

26 Col. 1:18.   27 Rom. 8:29.   28 I Pet. 1:20.

bore all those who in time and eternity can or should be members of His Mystical Body.

That was God's will from eternity, in Jesus' predestination and yours;

that was the ineffable plan that God decreed.

Again, how wonderful!

Mary, Mother of God and *Mother of Men*.

We need not cite here in support of that doctrine all the possible quotations from the Fathers and Doctors of the Church, all the arguments of theologians, both ancient and modern.

We merely mention the fact, lest we forget it—and what a neglect of duty that would be!—that

Mary, because she is the *Mother of God*, is the *Mother of Men*, our *Mother*, my Mother.

I have only to search my heart for proof of what I aver.

For, this conviction was planted in my soul with the grace of my baptism.

From my tender childhood—and I appeal to everyone's experience—

I have felt that she, to whom my own mother dedicated me, at whose feet she taught me to kneel,

was the Mother of Jesus and my Mother.

Besides, from many an experience I learned that to my faith, strengthened as it was by boundless trust, she answered with a love I cannot describe.

All Christians have had the same experience, however little they know who you are, *Mary*.

They feel that they can throw themselves into your arms and repose on your heart,

the heart of a true *Mother of Men*, because true Mother of God.

Children, youths, grown-ups, the aged, all, on their knees before your images, with one voice proclaim

that no mother can be compared to you,

Mother of God, Mother of Men.
Now, more than ever, a universal outburst of faith and love impels them towards you.
They know that amidst the unspeakable evils of our day they can no longer have hope except in Him who was born of you—and their hope is invincible—
    and in a filial abandonment to you, who gave us birth in Him.
O admirable Mother, lean down to your children, who are the fruit of your motherly heart!
Impart new warmth to that fruit so often chilled and drooping!
Refashion us to His image and likeness, who entrusted us to you!

What an enchanting thought! I am, then, the fruit of a twofold love.
First, God loved me; and that love, *Mary,* He planted in your heart. The union of your two hearts engendered in my soul the life of grace.
The Holy Spirit, the eternal Love of the Father and the Son, diffuses that life in me;
    but you, by your *fiat* and in the perfume of that *Ave,* which
    Gabriel spoke, gladly cooperate with Him.

It is ever thus; here on earth that mystery never ends.
You carry me ever in your heart, that I may receive that Spirit of my God, of Jesus, your Son.
Like unto a child, who, while abiding in its mother's womb, lives only by her, so do I really live only by dwelling in your loving heart. My every supernatural breath is there.
In the light of eternity, without you I can desire or long for nothing.
For it is by Mary's hands that all heavenly gifts, all virtues and graces are bestowed. Mary shares them with whom she will, when she will, and as she wills.
From your very own supernatural substance, that is, from your boundless love I draw, like milk to my soul, the grace which

nourishes, sustains and develops Jesus' life in me.
> You are fruitful, then, by nature, in giving birth to Jesus Christ;
> by your love you are fruitful, when you conceive me in Him.[29]
> Motherhood of the flesh, Motherhood of love!
> Two motherhoods that meet and complete each other!
> *O Mother of God and Mother of Men!*[30]

To enjoy all the benefits flowing from that ineffable mystery, I must remain devoutly attached to you, my Mother, Mary.
Each moment of my life, which you gave me in Jesus, must be sustained.
Prayer will effect that. What prayer?
The prayer of a little child at the breast and as yet unable to walk.
If I wish to know what you are, Mother, I must know my own great weaknesses,
> my inconceivable wretchedness,
> my complete incapability for anything good.
> I must renounce all pretension, all presumption whatever; all my pride of intellect, all my so-called virtues and merits.
> Because I feel so poor, so weak, so little, I need you, my Mother.

> Besides, with what trustful abandon I should have recourse to you!
> Can a child really fear to approach his mother?

It is precisely a mother's duty to communicate the abundant life which she possesses within herself to form and strengthen her child. You, *Mary*, have another part to play for me, besides giving me Jesus, the fruit of your womb.
You are so anxious for me to entreat you, to implore you, that I lay my needs before you in all simplicity.
Doing that, I know that I please you no end.

---

29 St. Augustine, *De Sancta Virginitate*.
30 Schryvers, C.SS.R. *Ma Mère*.

You are generous beyond measure, with a passion for conferring favors on those who have recourse to you.

> Love me, then, as much as you know how to love.
> It is a mother's peculiar nature to love.
> But, a *Mother of God!*

Cradle my soul in your arms, nourish it with your milk, that is, with that love with which Jesus, your Son, your first-born among us, is filled to overflowing.

> You know my needs, my soul's needs, my body's needs;
> you know better than I—Jesus reveals it to you—what is most helpful to my following of Him.
> Help me! that I may ever bless and love you more.
> Yes, that I may love you more and more,
> with a son's love; with a love wholly interwoven with the love with which Jesus loves you!
> To love you is, I know, also ever to love Him, Love supreme.
> I know, too, that, whatever I may attempt to do, you will always love me more than I love you, even more than I long to be loved by you.
> What blessing mine, to know that I live in you!
> and that through you Jesus from heaven communicates His life to me!

CHAPTER X. PRAY FOR US
ALL-POWERFUL SUPPLIANT

HOLY *Mary, Mother of God and of Men, pray for us!*
Mother of mankind, you abound in divine life for yourself; for us you superabound in grace.
In the dispensing of grace your part, Mother, is the consequence of the part you played in its acquisition.
True it is that Jesus, in glory, by means of His divine wounds, is our authoritative intercessor;
    the meritorious cause of grace, He obtains it by a title of justice.[1]
All God's gifts come to us through His merits.
But you, Mary, are the all-powerful suppliant, through whom every prayer reaches up to Him and every grace comes down.

All that we can expect from God through you, you have earned through fittingness,[2] by a title of friendship.
With the *fiat* of your Annunciation you began that sublime mission as God's Auxiliatrix in our behalf.
From that moment the Father of heaven made Jesus and you, as it were, a redemptive pair; you, of course, dependent on Him;
    but, in all of Jesus' mysteries, in every circumstance of His life, the Father always thinks of you two together;
    together you two labor to save men.
I have already considered how you are charged with dispensing

---

1 *De condigno.*   2 *De congruo.*

to men, not of your own doing, but by way of fittingness, the supernatural life which has its origin in eternity.
The efficacy of that fittingness touches all those to whom Jesus, the source of all blessings, applies His salvific causality.

That is especially true, when it is a question of your prayer, of the expression of your wishes, those wishes which present our needs—needs of body and needs of soul.
Because of your dignity, *Mary,* you reach to the borders of the divine.
He who gives grace takes your prayers for commands.
Now, we know that you wish God's grace for us—and with what fidelity, with what ardor!
God's incomparable delight, His Immaculate One, most pure, most beautiful, supremely pleasing to eternal Love,
> what can He refuse you?
> When the Persons of the Blessed Trinity gaze on you, do they see in you aught but Jesus Christ?
> and the treasure-house of all their blessings?

Everything which Jesus may claim in justice is yours by friendship's title.
The Doctors of the Church are right in saying that it is through your prayers and dignity that the power and the fruits of Jesus' Passion are applied to men.
No! a thousand times no! the fact that we present our requests through you in no way detracts from Jesus.
He is always necessarily our principal intercessor with His Father in heaven.
> All His blessed Passion, His ever-gaping wounds plead to God without ceasing;
> no intercession, neither yours nor that of any saint, is of value except through Him, through His blessed wounds.
> But, if it is true that in the task of redemption you cooperated with Him in everything,

in His joys and sorrows,
in His winning our salvation,
may I not conclude that you do the same in the dispensing of all the graces, material and spiritual, necessary for our salvation?

It is the opinion of great theologians, following those of saints and doctors, that no grace, none whatever,
even when I have recourse to a saint's intercession, comes from heaven to earth without having passed through your hands, *Mary,*
by your explicit mediation.
In full possession of your beatitude in heaven, Mother of all men, you whose motherhood, by reason of your dignity, your part, your relations with Christ, our Saviour, is so effective,
would you be completely happy, if in heaven you did not know the interests of those souls redeemed at the cost of so much pain, of Jesus' pain and your own?
All the blessed in heaven, it seems, have undoubtedly a right to such knowledge.
But you, Mother of God, yes, our Mother!
in order to give me the soul's life, to sustain it in me,
to develop meritorious acts in me, to destroy my vices, you have an obligation to know me thoroughly,
my thoughts, my desires, my dangers, my temptations, the help which I absolutely need to escape final shipwreck in this world.
That is the practical consequence of your motherhood.
Without it would you be the *Mother of God* and *Mother of Men?*

If, then, you know all that, since you see it, contemplate it in God, who discloses it to you as to no one else,
I cannot for a moment suspect, Mother all good, all heedful, all powerful as you are,
that you are unwilling to implore for me the graces which I

need so much,
and above all, to obtain them for me.

Some may say that on this subject opinions differ.
Perhaps so; but when we know that it is the practical teaching of Holy Mother Church in her sacred liturgy,
> when we hear avowing it a St. Germain of Constantinople, a St. Peter Damien, a St. Bernard—those illustrious Doctors of the Church—a St. Thomas Aquinas, prince of theologians, a St. Bernardine of Siena,
> an eminent theologian like Suarez among others, a St. Grignon de Montfort,
> a Bossuet, who preaches it in eloquent oratory,
> I repeat, it is most prudent, most consoling, most efficacious to believe it,
> with St. Alphonsus, who fills his "Glories of Mary" with it, with the theologians and doctors who followed him.

I quote Bossuet, because he sums up in wondrous manner the thought of the Church, of theologians, of the Fathers and Doctors:
> "God, having once decided to give us Jesus Christ by means of the Holy Virgin, does not retract His gifts. That order does not change.
>
> "It is true, it will always be true that, having through her love received the universal principle of grace, through her mediation we continue to receive its various effects in all the different states of Christian life.
>
> "Having by her motherly love contributed so much towards our salvation in the mystery of the Incarnation, the universal principle of grace, she contributes to it everlastingly in all the other operations which depend on that mystery."

Admitting that teaching which we felt it necessary to repeat, we understand now why the Church in her *Hail Mary* bids us fold our hands and cry out to the Mother of heaven:

Holy Mary, Mother of God, and necessarily, *Mother of Men, pray for us!*

That is the beautiful prayer which the *Hail Mary* puts on our lips.

I begin to grasp a little its power over the heart of a Mother who loves us!

All that we have written about the Angelic Salutation, about what it reveals to us of that Virgin and Mother, is nothing, absolutely nothing, in comparison to what it really contains.

To comprehend it fully, we should have to be Gabriel; better still, we would have to be God Himself.

Pray for us!

Who, when he recites that Ave properly, with full faith and trust and love, with at least something of that sublime respect which the archangel was able to put into it,

who does not feel sure, absolutely sure, of being answered? Of course, some souls, feeling too unworthy to be heeded, may not dare to pray to you like that, *Mary,* with that assurance.

Let them, then, place that *Ave* on the lips of Jesus Christ, the Son of God, your Son.

No one doubts that He, as yet in His beloved Mother's womb, sang that ineffable melody of the *Ave* to His Immaculate One.

Nor does anyone doubt that since then, on the lips of whoever has believed or will believe in you, He has continued and will continue to hymn that melody in a wide variety of accents of faith, hope and charity.

Mother of God, Mother of Men,
full of grace, the Lord is with thee;
blessed art thou among women,
thou, whose womb carried Jesus, the blessed fruit forever and ever!

He inspired the heavenly hierarchies with the outburst of admiration which they showed to you, Virgin-Mother,

when with Gabriel they repeated to you their *Ave Maria!*
The prophets, the evangelists, the apostles, who are Christ's glory,
the martyrs, whose crown He is,
the confessors, who honor His sanctity and live it, the heroic virgins, the chaste widows,
all the saints of God,
all those whose Queen you are,
all have learnt of Jesus that they must say to you:
Hail Mary!
All of them have repeated it over and over.
Only too well do they know that never, no never, do they say to you in vain:
Holy Mary, Mother of God, pray for us!
Following their example and striving to attain to their faith, joining in their admiration, in their intense pleading,
we, wretched ones, we, who are so in need of pity, in need only of your mercy, we cry out to you, *Mother of God,* our *Mother: Holy Mary, pray for us!*

Pray for us, you who are so powerful, in our behalf all powerful! You who know all our needs, needs of body and needs of soul, infinitely better than a mother, keen as she is, can discern them,
pray for us, for us who sigh to you in this vale of tears, that we may be comforted, enlightened, strengthened, sustained, guided, consoled, and finally saved!
Holy Mary, Mother of God, pray for us!

CHAPTER XI. SINNERS
MOTHER OF MERCY

H OLY *Mary, Mother of God, pray for us sinners*
On a feast of your Assumption, St. Bernard, the most illustrious of your panegyrists, addressed you thus:
"Through you, Mary, heaven has been filled;
through you hell has beheld itself robbed of an army of souls;
in a word, through you eternal life was imparted to multitudes of wretched ones, who had made themselves unworthy of it."[1]
That conviction, supported by all your saints, all your doctors, all your theologians, ancient and modern, has led us to implore you:
Pray for us sinners.

O, hope of those who despair,
safe harbor of those in shipwreck,
refuge and asylum of sinners!
You have too much pity on us unhappy children of Eve, the first sinner,
too much compassion on our wretchedness.
We know, and the Church reminds us at all times and in all places,
that you are praying for us always, that over and over you pray for us,

---
[1] *In Assumpt. B.M.V.*, Serm. 4.

that you feel that you never pray for us enough;
for, your zeal to guard us against evil cannot find satiety. *Holy Mary, Mother of God and of Men, pray for us sinners!*

Sinners!
Ah, yes! such we are ...
Who does not admit it, lies, and "the truth is not in him."[2]
That magnificent creation, which eternal Love was pleased to fashion out of nothing, constituted an admirable harmony.
Every part of it sang God's glory, all of it was directed towards Him, the supreme Beginning and End of all men and of everything made for man.
All at once, in that divine symphony three false notes offended God's ear and wrenched souls away:
  pain, death, evil.
  Pain, in the midst of a world created for love;
    death, which in its passing ruthlessly mows down all beauty;
    evil, for which from that time on man acquired a taste, for which still at times he has insatiable desire.
  What was it that happened?

Man was false to his trust; he refused to obey his Maker.
Eve ate the forbidden fruit; she presented some of it to her husband, Adam, who ate of the same.
Mortal sin, destroying in them the ineffable image of the Blessed Trinity, brought death to their souls.
  It destroyed their soul's life and delivered them to God's wrath, their souls, and those of all men past, present and to be, condemning them to everlasting hell-fire.
At the same time concupiscence, the source and occasion of sin, flung itself upon them and all their descendants,
  upon us, upon me.
  Ah! what a mystery! The Apostle cries out:
  "For, that which I work, I understand not. For, I do not that

---

2 1 John 2:4.

> good which I will; but the evil which I hate, that I do.... Unhappy man that I am, who shall deliver me from the body of this death?"[3]

> Within myself I feel my blood infected, carrying along ills, ills of body, and above all ills of soul;
> a rebellious blood, revolting against God, against men, against myself,
> a blood that sometimes from the cradle acquires frightful instincts for evil.

I feel myself consumed by original sin and its dread consequences. True, only through my first father, Adam, am I guilty of that sin, because I am of his race and blood.

But wicked concupiscence, flowing directly from original sin and inclining to evil, drags me along in spite of myself—although always voluntarily—to personal sins, sins that I know only too well are my own.

In fallen man there is a sort of threefold pulsation, a threefold seething of the vitiated blood flowing in his veins.

The first of these impels my mind to self-exaltation truly foolish and presumptuous; it is my pride.

The second urges my senses to hateful desires; it is sensible pleasure in its every degree.

The third is rebellion against God's law, the law forbidding me that abuse of liberty which insults Him; it is my arrogance.

> "Concupiscence of the flesh, concupiscence of the eyes, the pride of life."[4] They are what tyrannize the world, but surely they do not come from God.

Sinners.

Here we should take time to describe, analyze and brand each of those sins, which we call capital, those seven horrifying heads which the infernal serpent raises to excite and entice our physical and moral being to evil.

---

3 Rom. 7, 15 and 24.   4 John 2:16.

Suffice it to recall that I am eaten with pride, covetousness, lust, anger, gluttony, envy and sloth.

It is not always the same with everyone to the same extent or in the same measure.

This one or that is more often the victim of one or other of those unwholesome inclinations; often it is a matter of temperament. But in everyone those inclinations are strong; they wait on only one act of negligence, one lapse of attention, one presumption, temptation, or proximate occasion, to awaken, to fling themselves upon the soul and dominate it.

Each one has, perhaps, his own peculiar sin, his dominant sin, so to speak; be it pride, impurity or sloth.

Ordinarily it is that sin that brings all others in its train and forces us to obey it as slaves.

> *Sinners.*
> Ah, yes! who will deliver me from the body of this death?
> It is inevitable that my body must die, because I have death in my soul.
> Who will deliver me from that latter death?
> Who will deliver me from sin, that inveterate and insatiate murderer?
> Who will deliver me from eternal death, revive me, give me life forever?

> *Holy Mary, pray for us sinners.*

Immaculate Mother, you alone knew not shipwreck in the deep ocean of humanity's crimes.

You alone knew how to triumph over the old serpent and to crush his head under your immaculate heel.

> *Pray for us sinners.*
> We are the poor publicans of the Gospel.

I assure you that we dare not boast of anything.

Scarcely do we dare to lift our eyes towards heaven, for fear of

soiling God's eyes,
> or, in particular, your eyes.
> Not mine to examine my neighbor's heart.
> I look into my own and in all sincerity I cry out to you in my turn:

> "Have mercy on me, a sinner!"[5]

Mother and refuge of sinners, spurn me not, turn me not away, when I entreat you!
But, no! You will never turn away those who have recourse to your compassion.

> True, many there are who are far from their father's house;
> so many who fly from you, who no doubt insult you.
> But, are they not all your children redeemed by the blood of your divine Son?
> and by your tears?
> Yes, they are straying children, doubtless worthy of every chastisement.
> But many of them are ignorant; only a few of them, who knows? fully responsible!
> Are they not precisely for that reason more unfortunate?

> *Sinners!*
> I am sure that you love them still and in spite of their sin, and that in their farthest straying you follow them with your mother's gaze. Your heart watches over them tenderly.
> Mother of the guilty, yes, but also Mother of Jesus, their Judge,
> will you bear to have them still remain His enemies?

> Some of them, also, wish sincerely to be converted,
> to throw themselves at the feet of a priest and with folded hands ask pardon.

Those above all! help them to break their chains, to shake off

---

5 St. Luke 18: 13.

their human respect, to hope in the mercy of your Son.
   Obtain for them that deep conviction of faith, that unwavering hope,
   that He, Infinite Love, will be completely ready to welcome them, to take them in His arms and press them to His Heart.

   Sinners.
Remind us often, all of us, how He looked on Peter and caused him to weep bitterly;[6]
   how He called to Paul on the road, saying to him: "I am Jesus whom thou persecutest";[7]
   how He lured Matthew, the publican, from his counting-table, with: "Follow me!";[8]
   how He made Zacheus, the chief of the publicans, come down from his sycamore tree, and agreed to abide in his house;[9]
   how to the doubting Thomas He showed His pierced hands, and allowed him to put his hand into His sacred side;[10]
   how to the Samaritan woman He gave the living water of the Holy Spirit which cleansed her;[11]
   how to Magdalen He presented His feet to be washed with her tears, covered with kisses, anointed with precious ointment;[12]
   how, finally, to the adulterous woman He gave this absolution: "Neither will I condemn thee."[13]
All those, men and women alike, longed to be freed from sin, to repose on His Heart of merciful love,
   love, "which gives its Heart to the wretched."
So many other sinners, men and women, still are unwilling to come to Him!
Who will invite them and induce them to take the first step, so often the most decisive step? Who will lead them back to God?
   You, *Mary,* refuge of sinners;

---

6 St. Luke 22:62.   7 Acts 9:5.   8 St. Matt. 9:9.
9 St. Luke 19:1–5.   10 St. John 20:27.   11 St. John 4.
12 St. Luke 7.   13 St. John 8:11.

you! since to reach us, poor sinners, every grace must first pass through you.

Pray for us.
Pray for me; I need you so much!
I am so deeply conscious of my incapability for good of any sort. Like other men, I bear in my heart the original wound; that wound has opened other self-inflicted wounds which are hard to close entirely.
Place your gentle motherly hand on those scars which retain a morbid tendency ever to be reopened.
Do to me as you did to your Son, Jesus, when, taken down from the Cross, He lay in your arms.
    Let your mother's tears course down on my open wounds, to bathe them and wash them clean.
    Pour out on them your healing balm.
Disdain not to imprint on them the kiss which closes them forever.
Show that you are truly my Mother,
Mother to me, to all those who with sincere contrition cry to you in their *Ave:*
    Pray for us sinners!

You inspired that great confidence in Bernadette,
    the "Confidante of your Immaculate Conception";
    your much-loved child, was she not!
    She gazed on you, contemplated you, admired you in eighteen apparitions;
    and afterwards declared you so beautiful, so completely beautiful, that, if she could look on you just once more, she would welcome death.

But, it was not to be. She had received from you the mission to suffer, to be humiliated, questioned, misunderstood, and to remain always sick in a poor convent infirmary.

She had received the lowly, but fruitful mission of praying for those millions of souls who would come to Massabielle,
    and sing their *Ave, Ave Maria!*
    She was to linger in the racking tortures of a sickness which crucified her;
    there in her armchair, as if on her blessed cross,
    while to her very last breath she murmured still that *Ave,* ever her only prayer:
Holy Mary, Mother of God, pray for us sinners,
"and for me, a sinner, a sinner!"

    So do those die who belong to Jesus Christ:
    "Sinners ... sinners ...!"
They are perfectly and sincerely conscious that such they are, before one conceived Immaculate.
But she, meanwhile, accepting the homage of their humble confession, moulds them and transfigures them to her own beauty,
    to make them still more worthy of that of the most beautiful of the sons of men.[14]
    He came precisely to call us, sinners,[15]
    to heal us, save us, restore us to life,
    "reforming the body of our lowness, made like to the body of his glory."[16]

---

14 Ps. 44:3.   15 St. Matt. 9:13.   16 Phil. 3:21.

CHAPTER XII. NOW, AND FOREVER

HOLY *Mary, Mother of God,*
pray for us sinners,
now, and at the hour of our death.

Now.
That single word! and yet, what a wealth of meaning!
O Mary, pray for us, now, for it is the hour when we need you, when we need to feel that you are *God's Mother,* and consequently *Our Mother.*

Now!
That little word contains so much!
Now ... what is that *now*?

In its best understood meaning, the present life; my life on earth;
the time of my pilgrimage in this vale of tears;
the time "while we are in the body, we are absent from the Lord,"[1]
waiting "until he comes."[2]
I have hope that, when for me that time is ended, Jesus will reach down to wretched me,
that He will take me to Himself, that there, where He is, I also may be, and may abide with Him forever.[3]
Holy Mary, pray for us, now.

---

1 2 Cor. 5:6.   2 1 Cor. 11:26.   3 St. John 14:3.

You are with the Lord, whom you glorify in His glory on high.
You have been clothed in the glory of a blessed Assumption.
You were crowned and seated at the right hand of your Son, the *blessed fruit of your womb.*
Pray for us sinners, *now!*

So much do we need you!
You have such influence with the Heart of Jesus, your beloved Son! Obtain for us the patience, the courage and the love to persevere in this wretched life!
We are exposed to so many dangers of body and soul;
    so often we run the risk of losing grace and everlasting life!
Safeguard, encourage our efforts to earn that reward promised to those who believe and hope.
Root out from our souls the love of things that pass away, that so quickly cloy, and sooner or later crumble into dust.
Remind us often that we are "strangers and pilgrims" here below,
    that we may restrain ourselves "from carnal desires which war against the soul."[4]
Except for Jesus and you, what can sustain us in our hour of accounting?
    Pray for us,
    now.
A small word, clear, incisive, like a cry leaping forth, heard for the first time today ... *now.*
Now; in fact, even today!
Pray for me, Holy Mary, today, on this day just dawned.
I have had to tear myself from sleep, so often too short;
I have had to rise from bed or pallet, which I do not always have.
So many there are who sleep under the stars,
    like Jesus, the Son of Man, who had not where to lay His head![5]

Today, still today, *now.*

---

4 1 Pet. 2:11.   5 St. Luke 9:58.

I must take on myself the heavy burden of the day just beginning, with everything that fills it;
> the duties of my state, inevitable, monotonous, tiring, sometimes so illusive;
> that work, so necessary for a living, for providing a living for my own.
> I must take up again the burden of pain, worry, anguish, today, *now;*
> the burden of suffering, torture of mind, and worse still of heart.
> On certain days I feel myself, as it were, crushed, and already in early morning little able to continue...
> but, notwithstanding, in spite of myself, in spite of everything, I must be up and doing.

Now.
O beloved Mother, *Mother of God* and *Mother of Men,*
Mother to him who is at your feet, stretching out his arms to you,
pray for us...for me!
Pray for me, who plead with you, who await from you the help, the grace, the light, the strength, the mercy that your prayer can obtain for one who puts all his trust in you.

Now.
I like to recognize, in that *now,* the direct indication of the time of trial in which God, for reasons I see not, understand not,
> has placed me, and in which He keeps me.
> Here on earth each one has his own time of trial;
> sooner or later it comes, but come it will!

It must come; for, to enter into glory with God, I must know suffering;
I must experience the bitterness, the humiliation, the crucifixion of that time.
Through it I must learn to submit to God,

>   to crush my pride, to penetrate my heart with patience and resignation.
>
> I must learn even to love suffering, not for itself—that is impossible—
>
>   but to accomplish God's holy and adorable will; to conform myself to the sweet law of His love.
>
> I must learn to acknowledge that the state I am in, everything that happens, is the working-out of that love;
>
> I must with all my heart prefer that state to all other states which might be more agreeable,
>
>   but which come less from my God.
>
>   *Holy Mary, pray for us sinners.*
>
> Pray for me, that I may achieve, may realize fully that *now*.
>
> Pray that I may bear no grudge against my neighbor, that I may be of help to him, that I may come to love all those for whom God's will has become the only rule of life.
>
>   Most dear Mother, you passed through a time of trial;
>   you know what it is to suffer.
>
>   Are you not, above all, the Mother of Sorrows?
>
>   Was there one sorrow you did not experience, you who show me your heart pierced with seven swords?
>
>   *Mother of God,* pray for me, *now* and always,
>   and always more and more!
>
>   If I must suffer further, increase in me by your prayer the strength to bear my cross;
>
>   to carry it in following Jesus, in following you,
>
>   in following all the true servitors and servants of God's adorable will!
>
>   *Now.*
>
>   Yes, in physical suffering that assaults me,
>   in moral pain that torments my heart,
>   in duty that binds me at every moment,

in temptation that harasses me,
in deception that frustrates all my hopes,
in the frightening shadows in which I stumble,
in the horrifying nights that darken my mind,
that wither up my soul.

Now.
Pray, O good Virgin, only consoler of the afflicted,
pray for us, for all those who are undergoing their trial,
that it may be to them a luminous way, a grace replete with love,
which will carry them to God, lead them finally to complete holiness,
and prepare them for the glad entry into His presence,
now, and forever!

CHAPTER XIII. AND AT THE HOUR OF OUR DEATH

T HAT *now*,—life on earth, the present day, the moment that is passing,
that *now,* which hastens on without interruption, which to me is like a passing shadow, never slackening, but ever hurrying me on.
That *now*... it must end—there is no escape—at the hour of death.
Certainly, no one doubts that "it is appointed unto men once to die, and after this the judgment."[1]

And at the hour... Each one has his hour for passing on a sudden from *now*... that is, from time to eternity.
Holy Virgin, *Mary, Mother of God* and *of Men, pray for us sinners, now and at the hour of our death.*

That hour will come....
It comes, it hurries, it rushes in.
It makes no sound to warn me of its approach, especially as the evening of life draws near....
How swiftly all flies!
How everything here on earth crumbles away! How everything palls, wearies me!
It is useless to try to escape death's pursuit.
Each year that slips into the gulf of the past,

---
1 Hebr. 9: 27.

each month that ends, each day that passes into oblivion,
each vanished moment, like each tick of the clock,
and the seasons which die off, the harvests reaped, the beautiful flowers which in autumn fade away and abandon their soiled and withered petals to the breeze;
all, all disappears and returns to the nothingness from which at a stroke of God's hand it one day came forth.
I, too, am going to die; I am already dying....

For, what is this life, but an unceasing loss of the forces which govern it?
What is it, but the forced march towards that which we call by a word that pierces us, so ominous is it, so crushing!
death, bitter death!
Its hour arrives; always it comes sooner than expected.
It strikes for all, for every age, everywhere.
Death's pitiless hunger preys especially on infancy.
It strikes the growing child, regardless of his innocence.
It respects neither youth's beauty nor the grown man's strength.
It suffices for it merely to shake the frailty of the aged to cause them to fall like leaves of a tree that whirl in the void.

Not without reason from our tender childhood,
> from the day on which, with mother as teacher, we learned the archangel's *Hail Mary;*
> not without reason do we pray in that way:
> *Holy Mary, Mother of God,*
> *pray for us, now,*
> *and at the hour of our death.*

For some years we have prayed thus;
> twenty, fifty, eighty years have we repeated that prayer, doubtless in order to remind ourselves that we must die and be ready always.

That persistence in saying our *Hail Mary* over and over might well become tedious;

it might frighten us, who knows? it could discourage us.
That prayer at the end—after meditating on so many beautiful things before it—those final words of my *Ave* may seem in some way to cast on those wonders a shadow which may lessen their dazzling effect.
But, no! quite the opposite.
Try it; say the *Hail Mary* attentively and devoutly.
What charm in that *Ave!* What peace floods the soul! and how much more keenly we experience the truth of that cry of the Hail Holy Queen:
O sweet Virgin Mary!
Precisely to lighten all the fearsome suggestions of the *Ave*'s ending:
At the hour of our death,
do we say at the beginning admiringly and lovingly:
Hail, Mary, full of grace,
the Lord is with thee;
blessed art thou among women,
and blessed is the fruit of thy womb, Jesus.
And then, full of confidence:
Pray for us, now and at the hour of our death!

All the great mysteries we have recalled, meditated on and contemplated in Gabriel's *Ave*
were conceived and willed by God.
Jesus and *Mary* lived them,
in order to help us to live a good life, *now,*
and at last one day to die a holy death.

For that very reason, Mary, we recite the Angelic Salutation in your honor untiringly.
We must say it and repeat it to satiety in life, to be able tenderly to utter it with invincible hope, with ever-mounting love
at the hour of our death.
For, come it will, that solemn hour, in which I shall in no way

be able to meditate for long or recite my holy Hours,
> or read the many beautiful things said of you,
>> or write to edify others, to console them and encourage them to good.

But my *Ave!* For so many years, for so long a time that prayer will have so thoroughly purified and sanctified my lips!
> Those lips will have breathed such perfume from that Rose, they will have savored such sweetness from her blessed Fruit, that they will stay, as it were, fixed on that *Ave,* knowing only how to say *Ave, Ave,* and always *Ave....*

Dearly loved Mother, Mother of God and my Mother, when finally that hour is at hand,
> when I shall no longer doubt its presence,
> when I shall read on the lips of those around that the moment has arrived,
> when I shall wonder at the mysterious whispers of kindly souls assisting me,
> when that hour at last begins to sound, to remind me that it is time to go to God,
> to meet at last my Jesus, my Judge, face to face,
> ah, no! rather my Saviour—His blessed name means that—
> oh! Then, as you so often promised, be there, praying for me, *at the hour of my death.*

Be there, a tender Mother, who knows what it means to suffer, to offer me, as support for my spent and tossing head,
the comforting pillow of your immaculate Heart,
on which Jesus so often reclined,
on which He reposed at the foot of the holy cross,
when your loving arms embraced Him,
and your hot tears coursed down upon His purple wounds,
to cleanse and close them.
Be there; let me know that you are there, looking on me in your kindly way.

Let me know that you still hear me, that you are listening, ready to help me.

Let me still have strength to murmur:
Hail, Mary, full of grace,
Holy Mary, Mother of God,
pray for me, now... yes! now... for me...
and at the hour of our death!

O white Lily of the glorious and ever peaceful Trinity, shining Rose of paradise!
You of whom the King of heaven deigned to be born and nourished,
flood my soul now with streams of that grace of which you are full!
Pray for me, now,
and *at the hour of my death!*

It may be that I shall no longer be conscious,
or, withdrawing within my soul,
my eyes dimmed, unseeing,
my ears closed to sound of a voice,
my lips no longer able to utter a word,
it may be, I say, I shall suddenly feel myself ushered into God's presence, with Him my only concern...

Oh! then... and from this moment I make the pact with you... then, believe me, from the inmost recess of my being I shall call to you, with my final tears I shall implore you.

that I may breathe into your motherly ear inclined to my distress, a final *Ave...*
Ave... Hail, *Mary,*
blessed among women, among mothers,
Pray, now, oh! pray...
It is the hour... *the hour of our death,*
the hour of mine.

> Pray, *Holy Mary, Mother of God,*
> pray to *Jesus, my Saviour, my only hope,*
> pray to the *blessed fruit of thy womb,*
> that He may be propitious to me,
> that He may show me favor such as in the Gospel He showed all who repented and begged for grace!
> Since my exile in this vale of tears is ended,
> since it is the hour to pass from this world to God,
> from death, yes, from death to the life that is,
> show me, reveal to me your *Jesus,*
> that delicious fruit of thy womb, who destroys forever in me the morbid inclinations of the forbidden fruit and its punishment.

Let me gaze on *Jesus* as He was when you gazed on Him.
Tear from my eyes the veil which until now has hindered me from seeing His face.
Finally, make me ready, lead me into that eternal vision in which, I hope, I may never tire of singing to Him forever,
> with you, Immaculate Mother,
> with Gabriel, with the angels of the Lord,
> with my Guardian Angel, who is another Phanuel of God and flame of His love:
> *Holy, Holy, Holy is the Lord God!*

> My *Ave* will express fully all that I wish to say and ask.
> I beg those present, watching for my last breath,
> to recite it with me, with deep faith,
> with immeasurable hope,
> with perfect love.

I beg them to deign to supply for me, as I sink in death, all the homage, all the love which I would like to offer you in that hour,
> you, my Mother, from whom I have received all that I am and all that I possess.

And since that magnificent apostle of the *Hail Mary,*
>	your child of Lourdes, the innocent shepherdess, the lowly Bernadette,
>	since she is always at your feet in heaven, more and more enraptured than she ever could be at her blessed earthly grotto,

I implore her to obtain for me of you, Immaculate Conception, at my last hour
>	the favor of awakening in my soul those same admirable sentiments which filled her whole being
>	at the moment when, enfeebled and helpless in her armchair, that source of miracles, which cradled her agony,
>	you gave her heart the strength to repeat to you her final *Ave.*

She was a saint, a real saint; we know it today. And what a saint! Yet, she called herself a "sinner, a sinner."

Dear Mother, I am not in any way worthy to resemble her; but, at that hour, answer my prayer!
I know not when that hour will come;
I know not what kind of death will be mine; I know not any of the circumstances that may accompany it.
That is why, with infinitely greater reason than that maiden, your confidante,
>	as of today, as if I were at that final moment,
>	on which my eternity depends,
>	with full faith, with complete trust, with limitless abandon once more I cry to you:
>	*Hail, Mary... full of grace,*
>	*the Lord is with thee;*
>	*blessed art thou among women,*
>	*and blessed is the fruit of thy womb, Jesus.*
>	*Holy Mary, Mother of God,*
>	*pray for us, sinners,*
>	for me, a sinner, yes, a sinner,
>	*now,*

and at the hour of our death.
Amen.

CHAPTER XIV. AMEN

A*MEN.*
That Amen was uttered to the glory of God.[1]
Amen...
May all that I say in reciting my *Ave,* may everything it signifies, be believed, honored and glorified!
May all that it asks for, be obtained for time and eternity;
  for the *now* of this life passing away,
  for today,
  for this very moment that flits by!
May that *Ave* realize its triumph over us, over me, for the glory of Jesus Christ,
  for the honor of *Holy Mary,*
  Mother of God and Mother of men,
  at the hour of our death,
  at the hour of my death, mine, a sinner, a sinner!
  Amen!

How grateful I am to you, *Mary,* for having allowed me to meditate on the grandeur of that *Ave,* that incomparable prayer, companion of the *Our Father,*
  to write some few words about it.
Only too well I know that my thoughts and my written words scarcely do justice to the reality of your being so sublime.
They are merely crumbs collected here and there from the

---

1 2 Cor. 1:20

banquet-table at which your great servitors, your saints, your doctors and learned theologians regale themselves.

What does it matter? This meditation on the *Hail Mary* foreshadows,
> though from afar, that reality of you.

It gives me, as it were, a foretaste in this vale of tears of that towards which I am tending in faith, in hope, in endless love,
> the everlasting vision of God, the meeting with Jesus, your Son, the sight of your beauty, of you, the all beautiful.
> *Amen.* So be it!

> The *Hail Mary*... that beautiful prayer!
> What an exquisite antiphon!
> I am not surprised that the sacred liturgy is filled with it;
> that your holy Mass *De Beata* abounds in it,
> that it runs throughout my breviary...
> It pleased Jesus so!
> You, too, it pleases, O Mother. May it always be so!
> *Amen.* So be it!

The *Hail Mary*. A prayer which God spoke to a Virgin Mother, which He delivered not by man's lips, but by those of an archangel, one of the seven who stand before God,[2]
> a prayer, which the Most Blessed Trinity composed and gave to Gabriel to bring to an Immaculate Conception!

After the *Our Father,* spoken by Jesus, eternal Wisdom,
> can we truly compare it to any other prayer for holiness, depth, sublimity, efficacy?

Each time we recite it, we renew in the Virgin's heart that boundless joy which flooded her soul at the moment when the Son of God, Mary's Son, became flesh within her!

The *Hail Mary*. Surely we must realize now that that salutation is the heavenly antidote protecting the soul against the mortal

---

2 St. Luke 1:19.

bite of the serpent,
> of that serpent found in so many a statue and picture of *Mary*, whose head she crushes under her virginal heel!

What a veritable bludgeon it is, for smiting unceasingly that head which contrived and still unflaggingly contrives every plot attempted against the glory of God and of His Christ,
> against the honor of the Virgin Mother, against her Immaculate Heart,
> against the conservation and integrity of the Church,
> against the perfection of her saints,
> against the welfare of peoples, of society, of families, of individuals!

The *Hail Mary*. It is the nail driven by the woman clothed with the
> sun into the temple of Sisara, the enemy of God's people;[3]
> the millstone crashing on the abominable Abimelech;[4]
> Judith's sword severing the head of the impious Holofernes.[5]

The *Hail Mary* remains the sword ever brandished by the Mother of God and ever crushing schisms, heresies, every enemy of the Christian name.

With the Hail Mary she triumphs and always will triumph over Satan, the eternal murderer.[6]

> *Amen.* So be it!
> *Ave Maria... Hail Mary!*

Take, then, Christian soul, that sword with which you, too, may crush the hordes of hell;
> with which you may overcome all temptations, in yourself and in all those you love;
> with which you may accomplish marvels,
> perform miracles,
> heal bodies and save souls.

---

3 Judg. 4:21. 4 *Ibid.* 9:53.
5 Judith 13:10. 6 St. John 8:44.

If it is possible for you, never neglect to say your beads every day, and, if you find time, even the whole fifteen decades.

Be not afraid of distractions, provided you are willing to struggle against them.
Our heavenly Mother understands so well our weakness, our tired feelings, our weariness at times.
Hail Mary's multiplied never displease her.
She appreciates your murmurings of faith, hope and love.
Do your best. But, never give up your beads.
To carry them on your person... is that not as if you were saying them all day, all night secretly?
Keep them, at times, especially in time of trial, in the hollow of your hand. That is to clasp Mary's hand.

To conclude, keep this in mind, at least:
> do not neglect to say three *Hail Mary's* morning and night to *Mary, Mother of God* and your Mother, to thank the Most Blessed Trinity for having given us her...

We can report marvelous results from faithfulness to that practice,
> among those who suffer, who labor, who undergo pain of any kind,
> in body, in soul, in the midst of cares, to safeguard their interests, for time and eternity.

When we love someone, we cease not to remind him of our love, and always we love him more.
In saying *Hail Mary,* you will never deceive your heart, and above all the *Immaculate Heart of Mary.*
She is your *Mother...* Does not that say all?
Amen! So be it! Yes, altogether right, sweet and good that it be so.

About The Cenacle Press at Silverstream Priory

An apostolate of the Benedictine monastery of Silverstream Priory in Ireland, the mission of The Cenacle Press can be summed up in four words: *Quis ostendit nobis bona*—who will show us good things (Psalm 4:6)? In an age of confusion, ugliness, and sin, our aim is to show something of the Highest Good to every reader who picks up our books. More specifically, we believe that the treasury of the centuries-old Benedictine tradition and the beauty of holiness which has characterized so many of its followers through the ages has something beneficial, worthwhile, and encouraging in it for every believer.

cenaclepress.com

Also Available:

Blessed Columba Marmion OSB
Christ in His Mysteries

Blessed Columba Marmion OSB
Words of Life On the Margin of the Missal

Dom John de Hemptinne OSB
A Benedictine Soul: Dom Pius de Hemptinne, Disciple of Blessed Columba Marmion

Robert Hugh Benson
The King's Achievement

Robert Hugh Benson
By What Authority

Robert Hugh Benson
The Friendship of Christ

Robert Hugh Benson
Confessions of a Convert

Dom Hubert Van Zeller OSB
Letters to A Soul

Dom Hubert Van Zeller OSB
We Work While the Light Lasts

Visit cenaclepress.com for our full catalogue.

www.ingramcontent.com/pod-product-compliance
Lightning Source LLC
Chambersburg PA
CBHW030108240426
43661CB00031B/1340/J